Entrepreneurial Voices

Jeffrey Cornwall

Copyright © 2024 Jeffrey Cornwall
All rights reserved.
ISBN: 9798320255170

DEDICATION

To Ann

Thanks for keeping the dream alive.

CONTENTS

Preface
Introduction

Section I: Vision, Purpose, and Success
    1) Maggie and Matt Kuyper
    2) Johnathan Murrell
    3) Amy Collins
    4) George Seay
    5) Ryan Reisdorf
    6) Tyler Bedwell
    7) Peter Smith
    8) Mark Rubenstein

Section II: Perseverance while Dancing with the Market
    9) Tyler King
    10) Shawn Glinter
    11) Patrick Linton
    12) Carl Meier
    13) Travis Contreras
    14) Robert Riggs
    15) Todd Tietgens
    16) Adam Bedwell

Section III: Serendipity
    17) Ryan Pruitt
    18) Holly Rachel and Lena Winfree
    19) Grace Moore
    20) Skylar Faria
    21) Gordon Droitcour
    22) Josh Gilreath

Section IV: Youthful Exuberance
    23) Sarah Beth Perry
    24) Hannah Rodriguez
    25) James Richard and Ethan Akdamar
    26) Cassie Schreiner
    27) Asher Segelken

ENTREPRENEURIAL VOICES

28) Clark Buckner

Section V: In Search of Balance

29) Jen, Susan, and Jadon
30) Meredith Mazie
31) Matt Fiedler
32) Ian Miller
33) Janice Dotti
34) Tony Bakker
35) Craig Irving

Epilogue

About the Author

Preface

In the late 1970s and early 1980s, I was a graduate student at the University of Kentucky. In one of my MBA classes, Professor Andy Grimes introduced us to a recently published book entitled *Working* by Studs Terkel.[1] The subtitle, *People Talk About What They Do All Day and How They Feel About What They Do*, although a bit wordy, captures the magic of this book. Rather than the author telling the stories of what people do in their jobs and why it gives them meaning, he captures it in *their* words through hundreds of hours of tape-recorded interviews.

The book has more than one hundred fifty vignettes from people from all walks of life. It created a kaleidoscope of the heart and soul of our economic system, from an attendant who parks cars to an executive in an advertising agency to a steelworker who helped build America's cities.

Over the years, I have picked up *Working* and opened it to a random page. Every story captures the raw emotion of work. They fill my imagination with who these people were and what it felt like to do their jobs. In the early part of my working life as an entrepreneur, I found the stories to be a humble reminder of the human side of work. It helped me be more intentional about the jobs we were creating, the people we hired to fill them, and my responsibility to them and their families to start a business that could sustain their livelihood. Later, when teaching and mentoring young entrepreneurs, I tried to give them that same sense of stewardship toward the people they hired. Even if they never picked up a copy of *Working*, I tried to pass along its lessons about how a job is more than just a simple economic transaction. Jobs help define who people are and contribute to their self-worth and meaning.

For the past several decades, my wife, Ann, has encouraged me to write a similar book that would give the same intimate and emotional view of what entrepreneurs do as they start and grow businesses as *Working* does for workers. The world is full of books in which authors give their views about entrepreneurship. She felt that a book that gave a first-hand perspective on starting and growing a business would offer more profound, richer lessons. Although intrigued by her idea, I felt inadequate and overwhelmed by the thought of trying to do something even remotely akin to Studs Terkel's book. And, even if I could pull it off, I never perceived I had the time it

---

[1] Terkel, S. (1972). Working. New Press.

would take to conduct and edit the interviews, nor the resources to pay transcriptionists for the hours and hours of work it would take to move the stories from recordings to paper. So, the project sat on the back burner of my to-do list for decades.

And then, eventually, I retired. I was planning to spend my retirement dedicating more time to our grandkids and my hobbies, such as golfing, photography, and hiking. But Ann reminded me that I had one piece of unfinished business from my career: the book. Time was no longer a constraint, and technology took care of the challenge of transcribing the interviews (reasonably priced software can now create an amazingly accurate transcription of an interview in minutes). Also, through years of writing textbooks, teaching and mentoring entrepreneurs, writing a blog, and recording podcasts, I became more confident and comfortable talking with entrepreneurs about their stories—no more excuses.

From the very first interview, I realized the wisdom of my wife's persistent nudging me into this project. I realized that up until now, my conversations with entrepreneurs were just that: conversations. Quite honestly, sometimes I found myself talking as much as they did. Conducting interviews that focus on coaxing business owners to tell their stories in their own way describing what matters *to them*, was a completely new experience for me. Rather than coach, mentor, teach, advise, or seek a specific response that I was looking for, I just listened. I discovered that with just a little bit of prodding, most entrepreneurs are eager to share their stories and perspectives from their journeys. Even the entrepreneurs with whom I had been at their side for much of their careers shared things I never knew about their experiences as business owners. It was humbling to give voice to these entrepreneurs and allow them to share their stories and feelings about their entrepreneurial journeys in their own ways.

Too many books about entrepreneurs try to treat them as epic heroes. Although entrepreneurship can be full of heroic acts, in the end, most business owners are just everyday people. That is also the truth about entrepreneurs in this book. I want to demystify starting and building a business because we need entrepreneurship in this world more than ever. As the great economist Schumpeter[2] helped us understand, entrepreneurship is the engine that keeps economies evolving and moving forward and fuels the process of free enterprise. I hope these stories inspire

---

[2] Schumpeter, J. (1942). Capitalism, Socialism, and Democracy. Harper and Brothers.

others to take the leap and become another entrepreneurial voice.

I did not fully anticipate the impact of COVID when I began conducting interviews. I had no intention of COVID being a theme of this book, yet it pops up in many of the stories that the entrepreneurs in this book shared with me. For some, the impact of COVID and the policies enacted to address it were devastating to their businesses. For others, the effects of COVID challenged them to think about managing their businesses in new ways. A few even found opportunities in the disruption COVID created. I came to appreciate that for those of us who lived through it, COVID is equivalent to the Great Depression for my parents' and grandparents' generations. It was a transformational event in our shared history. As much as I would have liked to keep COVID out of this book, these stories are their stories. COVID changed the world for all of us and is an important part of the context for many of the entrepreneurs' stories.

When people asked me about my plans for writing this book, my standard response was that I wanted to include at least 100 entrepreneurs, if not closer to the more than 150 interviews that Studs Terkel included in his 760-page book. But the world has changed in the fifty years since Terkel published *Working*. Most publishers, especially those who publish business books, don't want epically long books anymore. And to be fair, people no longer want to read long books. I decided to limit myself to about thirty to forty entrepreneurs who are interesting people with interesting stories. Finding enough willing entrepreneurs who would honestly share their stories was not a challenge! The challenge was deciding on which stories to include. I tried to get some variety regarding the industry, business model, and stage of development of the businesses my interview subjects owned. I could have easily filled multiple volumes of this book with entrepreneurs from Nashville, where we live, but instead, I used some frequent travel points and Zoom to bring in entrepreneurs from across the country.

The process of writing a book like this is so much more than just turning on a tape recorder! The transcript of each interview often starts at well over 10,000 words. However, given the reality of book publishing today, I needed to keep my total word count to less than 80,000 words. To allow me to include enough stories to paint an accurate picture of everyday entrepreneurs required me to edit down what they shared. The trick was to keep my editing from taking the stories out of *their* words and putting them into *mine*. So, I only included the sections that capture the essence of each entrepreneur's unique journey. Indeed, the business model is the focus of the edited version of a few transcripts. But for most, it was something else.

ENTREPRENEURIAL VOICES

Many shared the challenges of keeping healthy relationships with partners, spouses, family, or employees while building their businesses. A few focused on entrepreneurship's impact on the business owner's physical and mental health. Keeping business and career aspirations in balance with the higher purposes of life was a theme I heard more than a few times. Several recognized the serendipitous nature of it all, the role of luck in finding success. Others focus on a relentless pursuit of a vision. All these things, and more, create the mosaic of everyday entrepreneurs. Together, the stories offer incredible lessons and insights about owning a business.

All the interviews have been reviewed and approved by the subjects. In many cases, they were an active part of the editing process. I promised them from the beginning that I wanted this to be *their* stories told in *their* words. I only included interviews that have the entrepreneur's full blessing and permission.

Finally, here are a few words of thanks. Ann Cornwall, Maggie Kuyper, Elizabeth Gortmaker, and James Richard all helped connect me with many of the amazing entrepreneurs included in this book. Thanks to Andy Grimes for introducing me to *Working* more than four decades ago. Thanks to all the entrepreneurs who created businesses around the technology and the software that made this project doable for a guy trying to ease into retirement. A special thanks to Jim Tarwater, a dear friend who happens to be a book collector, for inspiring me when I needed it with the gift of a "Special Advanced Proof Uncorrected" copy of *Working* that was autographed by Studs Terkel himself.

And, of course, my greatest thanks must go to my wife, Ann, for never allowing me to let the dream of this project fade away.

Introduction

There are thousands of books written by authors to help entrepreneurs. I've also written this type of book more than once. Although these books often include stories and quotes from entrepreneurs, they are all written from the author's perspective. Rather than create one more book in this mold, I decided to offer a different perspective. This book provides lessons, insights, and inspiration from entrepreneurs *in their own words*.

Although entrepreneurs have many things in common, they all have unique aspects to their journeys. It is the commonness that helps us learn from each other. It is the uniqueness that makes each entrepreneur's story so intriguing. Even after working for five decades in entrepreneurship, I never tire of hearing another business owner's story. There are always new insights to be gained and new lessons to be learned. I could have easily interviewed entrepreneurs indefinitely for this book. But at some point, I had to face the reality of the constraints imposed by the reader's attention span and the publisher's word count limits.

Before I begin sharing the stories of the entrepreneurs that comprise most of the pages of this book, please indulge me by letting me share a little bit about who I am, my own journey as an entrepreneur, and my motivation to write this book.

Looking back, I have never been quite sure where I fit within the business world. My career has included times when I've held positions in universities and years when I was a full-time business owner. Throughout *every* phase of my career, I have found writing to be an important outlet for me to chronicle and share what I have learned from my own experiences and other entrepreneurs I have met along the way.

Early Business Lessons

While I was growing up, business was the typical dinnertime conversation topic in the Cornwall household. One of four brothers, I was the only one with a passion for business. As a teenager, I learned about business by buying and selling stuff, often door-to-door. Selling did not come naturally to me, but I persisted. I also spent time in several family-owned businesses. My dad was not an entrepreneur at that time, although he eventually left the corporate nest and became an entrepreneur. He always had a strong interest in small business. He and his partner bought into or outright acquired struggling small companies. They would then try to turn them around by coaching up the founders or bringing in a new team to run the business.

I learned the most from one of the family businesses I was involved with, a marina my dad and his business partner bought, which was on the lake I grew up on in Wisconsin. My dad put me in charge of the dock, where I supervised and scheduled the staff. I was not even old enough to drive when I started working there. We sold gas, bait, and snacks on the dock and rented small fishing boats. I learned (the hard way) about the pitfalls of hiring friends and the importance of customer service. I gained essential management experience that I drew from throughout the rest of my career. The most profound lesson I learned was the need for financial controls. The person my dad and his partner hired to run the entire marina operation took advantage of their trust and the weak financial controls in the business. He earned large commissions by selling new boats. In his first year, he sold more new boats than anyone in the state. However, he did this by running a scam. He inflated the allowance he gave on trade-ins to many times their actual market value. This mistake cost my dad and his partner hundreds of thousands of dollars and led to the decision to get out of that business. I learned that to be successful in business, I needed to understand the numbers. That is why I chose to pursue an MBA in finance. I also learned that effective management was fundamentally based on the saying made famous by Ronald Reagan: "Trust but verify."

Tweed Jackets and Elbow Patches

Eventually, it became clear that my dad and I were not made to be in business together. We were too much alike. We both wanted to be "in charge," but ultimately, only one person can captain the ship. This is when I decided to get an MBA in finance to strengthen that part of my skill set further.

My wife, Ann, and I moved to Lexington, Kentucky, where I entered graduate school. As I completed my MBA, the economy went into a deep recession. This was when I first learned that life is rarely linear and rarely follows even the most well-executed plan. Instead, life is a series of opportunities to consider, most of which are completely unexpected. When I graduated with my MBA in 1980, it was a horrible time to start a business. Not only was the economy in a recession, but interest rates had soared. We were in what became known as a period of stagflation. A recession and inflation rarely go together, but this time they did. And the result was devastating to the economy. So, I decided to stay at the university and pursue a doctorate in business. Ann had a good job at a local hospital, so staying put in Lexington made sense.

After I completed the doctoral program, Ann and I decided to move back to Wisconsin, where I took a teaching position at one of the state universities. The economy was still reeling, so it still was not a good time to start a business.

Into the Wild West

By the late 1980s, the economy had improved, and I was starting to get the itch to get back into business. The opportunity to join one of my brothers, a physician, and his partner proved to be the right one to lead me back into the private sector. Healthcare was an industry that was becoming disrupted. Healthcare prices were out of control. Large employers were looking for solutions to the rising cost of providing their employees with health insurance. The innovation that emerged was called "managed care," which moved the decision-making about what care a patient would receive from the healthcare providers to the insurance company. It was the kind of disruption that was turning healthcare upside-down and inside-out. Like all disruptions, it was creating incredible opportunities for innovation. Entrepreneurs were finding that instead of fighting managed care through litigation and legislation, as many existing providers and healthcare organizations were trying to do, there were countless opportunities to start innovative healthcare delivery programs that met the needs of the new system of managed care. The specific target population that my partners sought to address was severely mentally ill children and adolescents. Traditionally, this population was treated in psychiatric hospitals, which were extremely expensive and not very effective. We planned to develop programs and facilities to get these kids out of the hospital and into lower levels of care that were much less expensive and proved to be much more effective. So, Ann and I moved our family, which now included two young children, from Wisconsin to North Carolina, where my new business partners had their medical practices.

Our business model proved to be just what the market was looking for. Our business grew rapidly, funded by cash flow, debt financing, and an investment from an angel investor. We grew from 17 to 175 full-time employees during our third year in business. In the subsequent fifteen months, we grew to about 350 employees. We built two significant residential campuses and leased office spaces in cities throughout North Carolina.

During this time, I learned a lot about the challenges of leading a high-growth business. I had hands-on experience with start-up businesses and business education that was focused on large corporations, but neither of these prepared me to lead a rapidly growing company. It was a roller coaster ride that led me to many 70-to-90-hour work weeks. I also discovered the toll such a pace of work took on me personally.

After several years of growth, we realized it was time to exit our business and get it into the hands of a company that could take it to the next level. We had grown the business as far as we could with our skills and resources. As I navigated the exit of our business, which ended up being a wild ride itself, I developed blurriness in the lower quarter of my right eye. At first, I kept it to myself and tried to ignore it, as I did not think I had time to see a doctor. But soon, it got to the point where I was having trouble driving, so I told Ann. Obviously, she was concerned and convinced me to see my ophthalmologist. He could see nothing structurally wrong with my eye, so he referred me for more tests. He suspected it might be the early stages of multiple sclerosis. Those tests came back negative, but what they found was that I most likely had a minor stroke. I was in my early 40s at that time. He suggested significant lifestyle changes, including getting any stress out of my life. We had just had two aborted closings during the exit of our business and were moving toward our third attempt. Get rid of stress? Easier said than done!

Eventually, we exited, and I began exploring what I wanted to do next. I was fascinated by the growing impact of information technology in healthcare. I came down to breakfast one morning and announced to Ann that I was going to launch a new business in healthcare tech. Ann warmly smiled and said, "That's nice, but you're in 'time out'—no deals for six months. If you still want to pursue this after six months, I will back you 100 percent. For now, you need to focus on your health and getting to know your family again."

Deep down, I knew she was right, but it was a hard message to hear. Over the first few days, I tried to negotiate with her, but she was firm. "No deals for six months."

I tried to fill my time with golf and consulting, but nothing brought me peace or contentment. I felt this growing sense of restlessness and anxiousness, which lasted for the first few months of my time out. Eventually, I began to feel calmer. I also noticed that I became more aware. I enjoyed taking walks with the family and just sitting on the back deck watching the birds.

One day, Ann said, "Have you ever thought about teaching again? After all you've been through, you would have so much to offer your business students." I assured her that I intended to get back into business when my six months were up. However, the seed was planted. A few weeks later, I came down to breakfast and announced that I was going to get back into higher education. Ann smiled and said, "That's nice!"

Tweed Jackets Redux

I discovered that during my decade away from higher education, universities across the country were starting entrepreneurship programs. I decided to take a position at the University of St. Thomas in St. Paul, Minnesota. They wanted to bring two of us in to reinvigorate one of the granddaddy entrepreneurship programs in the country. I focused on the undergraduate students and my counterpart, the MBA program.

One of the areas I focused on was managing growth. Entrepreneurship programs did a good job of preparing people to start businesses but very little to prepare them to grow and build their businesses. I wanted to better prepare future entrepreneurs for the growth-related challenges I faced while leading our healthcare business.

After six years, Ann and I decided we had enough of Minnesota winters. We decided we were ready to move back to the southeast. Belmont University in Nashville hired me to launch a new entrepreneurship program. Soon after we moved, our kids both relocated to Nashville, and it became home to our family. I spent the next several years building the entrepreneurship program at Belmont.

Eventually, I began to feel a bit restless again. I thought it might be time for a new opportunity. I explored some possible business ventures but found myself drawn to remain in higher education. One of the universities I was in contact with was looking to build an entrepreneurship program. They offered me a job to lead this effort. I was intrigued and felt it might be time for a new adventure.

Our family went to dinner that evening at one of our favorite spots, where

I planned to talk about the new opportunity with my family. Ann was already on board, but I had not shared my potential new beginning with our kids. Our son and daughter were married by now, and both our daughter and daughter-in-law were pregnant with their first children. I envisioned everyone excited for me, but I got something else! Instead, there were tears and confusion. I promised them I would not decide until I had thought it through some more.

I decided to make one more trip to the university that gave me the job offer, which was a few hours' drive from Nashville. I had a great visit and felt a renewed sense of commitment to make a change. But on the drive back home, I started thinking about my family's reaction at dinner and realized that it was time to stop "climbing mountains" and time to start enjoying "the valley." I went to my dean and told him that I was finished leading programs. I just wanted to spend my time doing what I enjoyed: teaching and writing.

A few years later, Ann, the kids, and I had started a small side business, which scratched my entrepreneurial itch. We developed an extensive catalog of video courses on small business and entrepreneurship. We've been marketing our content around the globe, often to nonprofits seeking to help people gain economic independence. What this business lacks in financial success it more than makes up for in the knowledge that we are helping people start new lives and help build their local communities.

Happy Trails

Eventually, time catches up with all of us, bringing me to the current phase in life. COVID had a devastating impact on higher education. I also started to work with a new generation of students, many of whom have learned in high school that capitalism and free enterprise are evil. Through all this turmoil, I realized I was getting just plain worn out. So, I decided to retire. I am not sure there is really such a thing as a traditional retirement for entrepreneurs. The pace has changed. I can do what interests me, not what a job or a business demands of me. No more worrying about making payroll, no more endless and often meaningless faculty meetings, no more working out our personal travel around the limitations imposed by a job.

On Entrepreneurial Voices

In retirement, I finally had the time to work on a project Ann and I have always talked about: this book! We've imagined taking Studs Turkel's timeless book, *Working*, and applying his model to entrepreneurship. In retirement, I had the time to conduct interviews with entrepreneurs and edit their stories. I can help entrepreneurs share the lessons *they* have learned from *their* journeys. By sharing their experiences and the wisdom they have gained along the way, I hope they can inspire others to pursue entrepreneurial careers. I hope their stories can, in some small way, help reignite the entrepreneurial spirit in our culture and our economy.

More than anything else, this book is a series of stories about learning. Some lessons are about business. More of them are about life. Each entrepreneur I interviewed shared their journey's story filled with "teachable moments." One of the entrepreneurs whose story is in this book, Sarah Beth Perry, said this about learning:

> "I just absolutely love that I get to learn so much and then create a process. Then, I get to teach someone else how to do it, hand it off, and keep learning new things. I think my favorite part about entrepreneurship is that I am naturally curious about a lot of things, and I get to explore new things on a daily basis. And so, today, I'm learning Facebook advertising. And then tomorrow, I'll learn how to take photos for a photo shoot and work the camera. Learning a bunch of different skills has definitely been my favorite part."

Successful entrepreneurs adapt their business models by listening to the brutally honest feedback the market offers. Those who listen to the market and adapt their business models have a chance of future success with their business. Those who stubbornly stick to their plan despite what customers tell them are often doomed to fail. Entrepreneurs learn new skills and knowledge with each new challenge they face in their business.

Entrepreneurs also learn about relationships. Entrepreneurship is a complex web of relationships with spouses, business partners, suppliers, employees, bankers, investors, and so forth. One of the first hard lessons many entrepreneurs learn is that the "being your own boss" part of business ownership is just a myth. Entrepreneurs are accountable to their customers, employees, investors, suppliers, and bankers. Entrepreneurship offers the chance to grow in our ability to work with others, develop our emotional intelligence, and balance the competing interests of our various stakeholders.

Along the way, entrepreneurs also learn about themselves. They learn how to deal with adversity and failure. They learn how to navigate seemingly contradictory demands. Sometimes, this learning about "self" can be an inspiring lesson of the courage and persistence they never knew they had in them. But other times, entrepreneurship can put a glaring spotlight on weaknesses in our character and breakdowns in our integrity.

From both the exciting and the difficult lessons, all this learning makes entrepreneurship an incredible experience. The lessons never stop, no matter how many years you've been in business or how many businesses you've launched. Even entrepreneurs in the later stages of their careers share stories of continued learning. I have seen my career unfold over the decades like a never-ending class on business and on life.

Finally, I have learned so much from the interviews I share in this book. I am truly humbled and honored that so many people chose to honestly and openly share their stories so that others can learn from them. I know I have!

JEFFREY CORNWALL

SECTION 1
VISION, PURPOSE, AND SUCCESS

"The best way to predict the future is to create it."
Peter Drucker

CHAPTER 1
Maggie and Matt Kuyper

Matt and Maggie both grew up with entrepreneurship in their families. After college, Matt pursued a career in commercial construction. Maggie started her work life as a high school teacher and volleyball coach. But eventually, the entrepreneurial spirit called out to both of them.

Matt: A friend of mine, and past client, owned a big commercial painting company in town, and they were looking for a new young estimator/project manager. That was my first introduction to the painting industry, and I really enjoyed it and made great connections. I did that for about four years. I really contemplated getting into the painting industry right out of that. I had a two-year non-compete that was not worth fighting. So, I went back to work in the construction project management field. After a couple of years of doing that, things just started falling into place. People were asking me if I was going to start a painting company, and crews were coming in asking if they could come to work for me. I didn't want to jump all in, so I started dabbling using the subcontractor model, where I was pricing and selling work and letting the subcontractors do the work.

I was doing it nights and weekends, and thankfully, my job was pretty flexible. I did that for over a year and grew Harpeth Painting quite substantially as a side business.

Maggie: We were pregnant with our third child. And by that time, you had told your current employer about Harpeth. It was just on the side at first, but when it became obvious that it was a thing, you gave them the heads up that it was in your trajectory to do your own business full-time. Three or four weeks before we had our third kid, you officially resigned, which I think to most people would be terrifying. But to us, it was perfect. I mean, you had control over your schedule and freedom for your family. Although, the day our son was born, you went to bid on a job while I was still in the hospital!

I was pretty involved in the back end of the business as soon as he went full-time. I was doing job costing, financial reconciliation, and just making sure things were paid and our ducks were in a row. When the residential side of the business started picking as much as the commercial side, Matt couldn't handle it all. So, we got part-time help for the baby, and I started dabbling more in Harpeth. I was thrown into selling residential work. And then, about a year after we took the business full-time, we were so overloaded that I ended up taking on a bunch of Matt's larger clients and getting thrust into new construction and big projects. I never really looked back.

Matt: I don't even know if we really had an official conversation. We didn't have any check-ins on "Is this okay? Are you doing okay? Is this trajectory okay?" But it wasn't like a sit down of, "Hey, this is going to be your role. This is our three-year plan." I mean, eventually, it got to that. But in the early phases, it was just, okay, now do this, and then do that.

Maggie: And the question was always, if one of us doesn't do this, we'll lose an opportunity. So, one of us was always, "Okay, let's do it!"

How do you navigate working together as a married couple?

Matt: Boundaries and communication. Boundaries in the sense that you need to develop or establish times when we talk about work and when we don't talk about work. Boundaries of how our roles are different at work versus how they're different at home. And communication to make sure we're on the same page.

Maggie: I got really good advice quite recently. We'll often sit on our porch and talk. It is a great time to decompress. Sometimes, it's big-picture work; sometimes, it's logistical; sometimes it's life. But the question I try to ask myself before I bring up anything work-related to Matt outside of work hours is, "Am I bringing this up because I don't have anything else to talk about, or am I bringing this up because I need to process it?" And that, I think, for me is good because I like to talk. If there's silence, I'll just talk. I'm learning to process if it is something that I need to process with him and get sorted out or if it is just because we're sitting on the porch and I feel like I need to talk.

Matt: In the early, more gritty years of the business, it was a lot of just my decision.

Maggie: You had the experience to make the decision.

Matt: And I'm a little more calculated. I'm not a risk-taker, but I'm a more risk-tolerant person. And that served well in the early greedy years. But as Maggie has officially taken over more of the executive leadership role of the company, I've had to make fewer decisions on my own because she has the goal of the whole company in her control. So, I've relinquished some of those decisions as roles have changed.

Maggie: Our leadership team was relieved to have a clear leader. We forget that there's probably something very intimidating about a married couple being jointly your boss. And there's some trepidation of handling something with a married couple versus handling something with a CEO.

I would say we still agree on most decisions. We've worked hard on a healthy marriage. Therefore, we're on the same trajectory.

Matt: And setting the goals for the business together. Strategic planning aligns for both of us, so that makes decisions for the business easier.

Maggie: And the core values of the company. We still go back to revisit those.

***

Maggie: We've had a lot of conversations recently about having a clear definition of our value proposition, and not in a chintzy sales way, but in a strategic way of what truly is setting us apart. The more we can answer what we offer, the more we can dig into our ideal customer. They go hand-in-hand.

One of the conversations we've had is, has this all just been a fluke? As we're digging into what is this value proposition, there's also a part of us that wonders if it's just kind of a happy accident, which isn't true.

Matt: One thing we're learning is that because we offer a wide variety of services, we can serve a customer across a lot of different projects. Our high-end residential market brings value to our commercial clients when we have unique applications, fancy wallpaper, or some high-end finish in a commercial building. And our production mindset from our commercial experience serves as well when there are hard deadlines on a residential project.

Maggie: I think another thing is, and I don't know that we've ever used this word, but I think there's a humility across our culture that serves our clientele very well. We're not pushy. We're not know-it-alls. We're very team-oriented, and that's a breath of fresh air on top of being able to do a bunch of things. It's comforting for our clients to know, "Wow, they're capable, and they're really enjoyable and nice to work with.

Would you like it to become a second-generation family business?

Maggie: I hope one of them takes over. We tried to get Lucy [the oldest of their three children] involved early on. We had her clean the shop once a week. I gave her a very generous offer: $20 a week to clean the shop.

She did it twice. And when I say she did it, I think she wiped the toilets, mopped the bathroom floor, and called it good. It is a 3000 square foot shop! My intuition quickly kicked in that this is this is a real fast way for her to hate Harpeth Painting. So, we pivoted from that. And right now, our focus has been not making the kids resent our company because there are times that we're busy and work interferes with family time. Right now, it's more about helping them understand what is work and why work is good. They love getting to know the people in our company. We're giving them little tidbits of what it's like to own a business. And then, as they start to learn their gifts and talents, we might see if it folds into little random task jobs or lessons.

What's cool in our industry, and this is true of a lot of trades, is it's not all about money. You can do very well, even as a craftsman. Even if one of our kids wants to learn how to paint, they could have a great career doing that. And it's cool that we're able in a culture where kids are taught that they have to go to a college that we can either do that for our kids or show them another option.

I want our girls to be able to grow up and know that it's fine if they want to have a career or it's fine if they want to stay home. I hope there's an entrepreneurial spirit within them, even if it's within a corporate setting or whatever they end up doing. I want them to think critically like they saw us doing.

Harpeth Painting has experienced significant growth. What are your plans for its future?

Matt: We back into revenue growth from a net profit perspective. We're not fighting a top-line revenue number. If, at some point, it doesn't make sense for the revenue to be a certain thing and the profit to be another thing, then it doesn't make sense to grow.

There's no track record. We're already in the top 0.1% of painting contractors and probably the top 1% of entrepreneurs in general. So, there's not a lot of data points and information that we can gather that tells us this is the sweet spot of where we need to be. We're learning that as we go.

Maggie: Like Matt said, we enjoy it. We want to have a little bit of bandwidth to diversify ourselves. One of our biggest fears for both of us is being "all in." What if something goes crazy, whether internally, legally, or in the world. All our eggs are in one basket right now, which has thankfully been fine. But as we grow and stabilize, we want to have some capacity to diversify a little bit, which you can't do when we both work 40 hours a week, full-time in the business.

It's only been a year and a half that we've really paid attention to strategic growth. We're still gathering information. I mean, we didn't start job costing until three years ago. And so, we don't have a ton of back data to make decisions strategically. We know what we think this next year is going to be. And if it works, and we hope it will, then we'll be able to make a strategic decision about the size we want to get to and what it looks like.

Every time we've grown, it's to better serve our favorite clients. We did an exercise with the team where everybody had to list their top three favorite clients. The reason we've grown is because they're growing. Our growth has truly been to continue to serve the needs of our people.

Chapter 2
Jonathan Murrell

Jonathan and his siblings grew up in the Philippines, where their parents were missionaries. Jonathan and his brother James both had an entrepreneurial spirit since their youth. The two brothers enrolled in colleges in Nashville, TN that were only a few miles apart. When they graduated from college, they owned a wholesale candy distribution company that leased a warehouse and employed several people. Soon after college, they decided to exit the candy business and find a new opportunity. A family friend from their church approached them about joining him in launching a business he had experienced in Europe: escape rooms. At the time there were only a handful of escape rooms in the US. After flying to Europe to see escape rooms firsthand, the three decided to launch The Escape Game. Within the first few months of operation, their first store became rated the number one thing to do in Nashville on TripAdvisor.

The TripAdvisor wave carried us through the first launch. We didn't start the business with a grand scheme to grow. We started the business thinking this is really unique. There is no analog. There are no national brands. There are no global brands. There is no company that has more than two of these in the world right now. That's where the world was in this industry at the time. We said, "Let's do one; let's do it really well. Let's see what becomes of it." TripAdvisor really helped launch that first store. And then three months in we said, "This is going so well. We have to do more of these."

We pursued a second location and opened location number two roughly a year after the first one opened. TripAdvisor was still a major part of that location. By the time we got to around location three or four, TripAdvisor did the first of many dreaded algorithm changes where they decided, "Oh, it's a little weird that in every city in the world, the number one thing to do is an escape game." At some point, someone at TripAdvisor decided that that didn't accurately represent the way they wanted to show the world. And so, they created a new category called "Fun and Games." They split us out. It really was driven by the dominance of escape rooms as a sector. And so, they started to get more refined in the way they approach their own search results. They now said there's things to do, and fun and games is a thing to do. You have museums, cultural tours, biking tours, and fun and games as categories now. We immediately were the top ranking in the fun and games category, but we no longer had that top level visibility from TripAdvisor. That immediately changed the flood of guests we were getting from that channel.

Fortunately, at that point, we had we had already begun the journey of saying we want to get good locations and we want to be the most premier thing out there. Traditionally, escape games were viewed as destinations you could play if you were going to book in advance. We had this bold moment where we went for the big, bold one on the prime street in Orlando's tourism district versus the two other locations we had that were dramatically cheaper and more destination focused, which would have been considered normal for escape rooms at the time.

Our strategy is much clearer in hindsight. A series of fortunate decisions /opportunities later we found ourselves with several very high-profile locations that saw a tremendous amount of foot traffic. This made us realize that Wow, the location itself can be a driver. When TripAdvisor pulled the rug out from under escape rooms, we already had a real estate strategy that allowed us to be a stand-alone entertainment venue. We weren't dependent solely on that one funnel at the time. We also need to go where people are naturally congregating, go to good locations where they're going to feel comfortable coming. We need those reviews because they still matter, just not quite as much as they did. This sort of three-pronged strategy started to emerge, which was to serve guests really well to get great reviews and feedback and create word of mouth, build really great games that supplement that, and put them in great locations. And that sort of started to become the way we approached the business and that began to inform our growth and our strategy.

Go back to when you had one store. What was a typical day for you day-to-day?

For the first four months, we were only focused on the one store. It was seven days a week. Either me or my brother would open the building and close the building seven days a week. We had a very small team. I was doing bookkeeping, accounting, paying bills, and designing the new games. As we grew, I'd usually spend the morning building and working on games and in the evening running games and repeat, repeat, repeat, repeat for the first four or five months, just sort of running at a million miles an hour, sleeping very little.

When we started working on location two, I started spending more and more of my time focused on how we were going to build a store in Orlando. Now there's all this pressure because in the intervening year, several hundred escape rooms opened. Now there's all these points of comparison and competition, and an industry was beginning to emerge.

ENTREPRENEURIAL VOICES

We've got to deliver a better product. I was working largely on any kind of back of house things for the first unit, but then really working on what does this mean to build the second one.

I was trying to figure out what to do. It started with trying to figure out how to look for real estate and how to find a broker in Orlando that we could work with. I started interviewing architects to find architects we could work with. The first store in Nashville, just like most escape rooms, we just kind of move furniture around and put locks on things. But by the time we were going to number two, we were wanting to approach it from a much more sophisticated perspective. I remember spending my day interviewing builders, interviewing craftspeople, art companies, because we didn't have any of those skills in house. I had no background in these things and trying to figure out, basically piece by piece, how could I build an immersive escape room using this vendor network. How do you launch a store in another city? How do you hire in another city? I mean, every morning I'd just wake up and excitedly tackle a problem that I didn't know existed the night before. And the deeper I got, the more I realized that we did not know very much.

I often think if we had known how many hills and like how many valleys and how terribly challenging this journey would have been, I don't think we would have willingly gone on that road. But we excitedly, naively rushed headlong into trying to build a retail business.
We were trying to build a manufacturing business and a retail business simultaneously. Those are two really hard things. Most people do one or the other. And we had to do both, and we had to learn how to do both really quickly. Looking back, I think it was harder than we realized.

So where do you think this is headed?

Today twenty-six locations have opened. Four more will open this year, so we're going to end the year with roughly thirty stores. We already have ten deals identified for 2023. We have a pretty clear vision as a company of this path to fifty stores opened. Our mission is to define and dominate the world of escape rooms and then disrupt the world of entertainment. We feel like we've done a good job defining the industry of escape rooms. At this point in our scale journey, we're the largest gross revenue operator of escape rooms in the country. More people say that they started their business or modeled their business after our brand and our approach to guest service game quality, so we feel like, in the humblest way possible, that we've really done a good job defining the space.

We see ourselves in this transitional stage from going from trying to be the best dominant player in the escape game category to trying to be seen more as a true entertainment competitor. We're going up against Punch Bowl Social and Dave and Busters versus being relegated to sort of a small niche of mom-and-pop operators who don't really know what they're doing. We feel like when we hit that fifty-store mark with close to $100 million in revenues, it's going to be hard to treat it like a side category anymore. We're going to be seen more as a national entertainment company and continue to grow from there.

Is this something you want to see yourself doing for another ten years?

In 2018, at about the year five mark, we brought in private equity partners. We're approaching the conversation around who the next equity partners will be, as their lifecycle with us is coming to an end. We'll end up with new equity partners. I'm really excited about doing this one more time with the second set of partners. I'm really excited for this next round we're about to go through to see the next evolution of The Escape Room. We went from eight stores to forty stores in five or six years. It was a really cool roller coaster ride! I think that this journey with the next group of equity partners going from forty to 120 or even 150 units is going to be super exciting. I'm very interested in going along for that ride and learning on that journey from people who've taken companies through that stage. And then there's a part of me that wonders once it gets bigger than that, if the size and the potential bureaucratic implications of that size will just start to drive me crazy. And I wonder if I'm going to be better suited to a middle market company than a larger company.

What was your best day over the last eight years?

It's hard to say any day other than when we brought in the private equity partners, because it was a very exciting culmination of the first four and a half years of really hard work. It was the open door to an incredible opportunity to learn from people who've done this before, across all industries and categories. That transaction day was very satisfying and amazing. But you know, sitting back as we're about to do the whole thing again, you look back and say, "Oh, wow! In the early stages of 2018, you had eight stores. By 2023, you're going to have 40 stores. You had 250 employees. Now you have 950."

The last four years have had huge swings of momentum. In that period, we had at least three major restructures. We ran out of cash twice. We recovered from COVID, after being totally shut down for months at a time. There were at least two moments during that period where we weren't sure if we would be an existing company. You can paint a very straight linear line of going from 8 to 40 stores. But it's actually been four and a half years of like ups and downs and all over the place. Yeah, a lot has happened.

What was the worst day?

The private equity company wanted a non-founding CEO brought in. They put together a growth plan that was overly aggressive. In the first 18 months, we tried to double store count instead of a more measured pace, which led to bloated overhead across the company. Headcount went from 30 at headquarters to 130 or something over 14 months. A crazy hiring spree outran cash too fast. We had to step in and do a major restructure and let go of maybe 40% of the headcount that had been hired in the last 14 months. It was so frustrating and really hard to do that, as they never should have been hired to begin with. It was just completely, ridiculously bad management and decision-making that led to us having to do that. It was the original founders who had to step in and do that hard restructure.

About five months later, we wound up letting that CEO go because we still had not changed enough. Then came another round of restructuring. We did the deal, had an eighteen-month growth spurt, and grew out of control, and then the founding team had to come back through and do two major restructures spaced about four months apart. We had to gut the business back to what was a sustainable size, cut working capital expenses, change growth plans down to a reasonable size, and raise additional debt funding to move us into the future. This period of three months of course-correcting the company was chaotic and challenging but also very refreshing because it finally felt like we were regaining control of the thing that had kind of gotten out of hand post PE transaction. It felt like the thing had kind of run away from us but was now back under control. It was a strange mix of simultaneously refreshing and terrible days. These were terrible days.

Mark, one of the three founders, became the CEO. We were all on board and aligned and then had our best quarter ever. And then COVID hit. We had 18 stores open, all 18 stores had to shut down, and COVID did its thing. But we made it through.

Imagine that you're an old guy. What would success look like to you when looking back on the kind of career that you've been describing?

I've been wrestling with that question a lot lately. The way I prioritize my life now and will always prioritize is faith and family first. And then friends and work. Keeping those first two priorities as my top priorities for the next 50 years, I'll look back as a success. I've been fortunate to where I don't need to work anymore. But I always feel like I'll never be able to retire. But for me, I like to create things because it gives me opportunities to give things away. And so, I think for me, really that's a prime motivator. We've been able to start a foundation after the private equity deal a few years ago. Spending time on that and doing that work motivates me to do my day job better because if I can make The Escape Game bigger, the foundation can be bigger. I don't like buying things, I don't spend money on anything. The money itself is not really a good motivator. Putting it into my foundation does.

We disburse to a number of causes but one of my favorites is a charity in the Philippines, where I grew up, that serves underprivileged kids, getting them through school. And we do a lot of work with churches around the world in very poor and impoverished countries that are serving their communities. My work now is influenced by the fact that I grew up in a very poor country and saw how education can completely change the trajectory of someone's life.

Chapter 3

Amy Collins

Amy started in nursing but caught the entrepreneurial bug. She took her grandmother's cinnamon roll recipe and launched RoRo's Baking Company with her grandmother and husband as partners. Their products are available in stores across the southeastern U.S.

My grandmother had sold her rolls around the community, at school bake sales, and at church fundraisers. I remember my parents sitting down in the kitchen with her, I think I was in high school, and having a conversation about opening a bakery and selling her baked goods. And so, that was kind of always in the back of my mind.

When my husband and I got married in 2010, she baked over 200 favors for our wedding. That was kind of the start of it. People would go crazy for them. We were like, we should see if this is something that we could sell!

I remember being really nervous. We approached my grandmother (Rochelle) and my late grandfather (Ken). She was 74 at the time. I still remember sitting in their little home office, and they said, "Yes, absolutely. This is something we've always wanted to do! We just never knew how to do it."

They were so excited. That solidified the original partnership of the four of us, which became three of us after my grandfather suddenly passed away about a year after our initial conversation. Her "grandmother name" is Roro, which was the name we came up with for the company as they are all her recipes. She just turned 85 and is still an owner of the company.

I paid the girl who did our invitations for our wedding something like $35 an hour to create some designs for our logo. We had a vision for what we wanted to look like. We wanted something classic and something that would withstand years and years. I still absolutely love the logo to this day. I researched starting an LLC, filing with the Secretary of State, getting an assumed name certificate, and opening up a bank account. I just started doing all of the little tasks that you have to do to start a business.

We found a commercial kitchen that we rented hourly near my grandmother's house and started buying ingredients -- not in bulk. Originally, we were going to Walmart and just stocking up on the biggest bags of flour we could find.

I thought we were going to sell in coffee shops. I remember going around to coffee shops, and everyone was saying, "We want really big cinnamon rolls." Ours were smaller and in a pan. It wasn't the reaction that I thought would happen right out of the gate.

Our first retailer was a small store called Celebration Market here in Dallas. The opening order she placed was for 12 pans and we were ecstatic! I think we burned more than half of that initial bake we did for this order as we were still learning how to use the equipment in the commercial bakery. But we thankfully got her 12 pans, and she ordered again the following week!

I ended up meeting a friend of a friend who worked in a high-end retail chain called Central Market here in Texas. They put me in touch with the frozen buyer, and she agreed to meet with me in the store. She loved our product. By the end of the meeting, she walked me over to the shelf and said, "Okay, here's where your products are going to go." That buyer really helped us and believed in us. She set us up with a distributor. We learned the grocery and distribution world. We were really careful that we just wanted to focus on one item, our cinnamon roll, and figure out what we were doing, and learn how to scale it.

There was a ton of trial and error and a lot of mistakes. At one point, we stored the ingredients in grandmother's unused shower, just stacking bags of flour and other ingredients. We were shrink-wrapping our product on her dining table and storing the frozen rolls in her garage.

I was still working full time as a nurse. I would do three nightshifts in a row then turn around and meet them at the kitchen on a Saturday morning. My husband was also working full-time. My aunts, uncles, and cousins would all be there, and we didn't pay them. They just helped.

We spent a lot of time educating people about who we are as a brand and getting them to try them. We found that once people tried them, they loved them, and then they told their friends about them. That was our biggest key to growing. We only focused on that one account. There were eight locations at the time, and they were pretty high volume. We are proudly still on shelves 12 years later and they sell a ton of RoRo's!

Over the next couple of years, we ran the business in that shared-use commercial kitchen and overtook my grandmother's home. My grandmother was like, "I can't work like this anymore. We have to get a place of our own. This is crazy! We need space!"

We found a space in the Lakewood area of Dallas, and my grandmother helped fund a huge renovation. We did all the build-out. I became the general contractor. It was a 1,400-square-foot facility, and it felt huge and scary. Our rent was $750 a month, which was also overwhelming at the time. We dove in and believed we were selling enough that we could handle all of the expenses. It allowed us to grow.

We went into some other mom-and-pop stores. Eventually, we went into the southwest region of Whole Foods and H-E-B. We got to about 300 stores very gradually over about ten years. I didn't dive in full-time until the summer of 2021. And since then, we've really started to grow.

In between all this, we had a lot of personal things going on, too. In 2018, I had my first daughter at 23 weeks and three days. That halted our life for about a year and a half. She had a five-month NICU[3] stay, and then a year of intense therapies. At that point, I was not in a headspace where we could focus on growth. She's amazingly a thriving, wonderful four-year-old now.

When she was home, and we knew she was going to be okay, we started doing a lot of influencer partnerships and marketing. It just kind of fell into our lap. We started sending boxes to people who had a large following on Instagram and who were excited about the product. Our visibility grew so much during that time. After she was home in 2019, we really started to focus on growth and getting a game plan together for how we were going to scale.

I knew we had a great product, but I also knew that my skill set wasn't in running a manufacturing facility. I had been counseled by a couple of other brands that you can either run a manufacturing facility, or you can grow your brand. I realized that I couldn't do both and wasn't good at both. We were still in our 1,400-square-foot facility. It took us a long time, a couple of years really, to find two different companies that would manufacture our products and that wanted to grow with us.

2020 was a really difficult year for food businesses that sell direct to

---

[3] Neonatal Intensive Care Unit

consumer. We stayed open, as we fell under, I don't know even how they worded it, the "necessary business" label. As it turned out, 2020 was our best year of growth ever. In 2021, we maintained that same pace.

We signed on with a national brokerage team in 2021. We had a plan for going outside of Texas, expanding the brand throughout the Southeast. I had been taking a small salary for the previous two years, and I felt like it was okay if I didn't have my nursing income anymore. I had my second daughter in 2021, and I decided that the business had grown to the point where we felt confident that I could dive in full-time. It just felt very scary to quit a nursing job to run a food brand when you have two young daughters. Even now, I'll lose sleep at night over costs and all of that stuff. It's because it's a labor-intensive item, and we are competing with national brands on shelf space. But we've always figured it out, and that's what I have to remember. We've always stuck with it, and we're now beginning to see the effects of that.

I've said to many people that it feels like a startup again since 2021. We've kind of figured out exactly who we are as a brand. We figured out a way to produce it. It's not necessarily that we're done with all of hurdles by any means. I feel like there are a lot of aspects that you have to figure out to get ready to grow it outside of your region and grow it nationally, which is what we're in the process of doing right now. It's exciting, and I think it's something that I will always be learning from. It will always be scary. One day of the week, it will feel like this is the best thing ever, and the next day, it feels like we're going to go out of business. It's just a constant roller coaster of emotions!

I was just accepted into an accelerator program called SKU, and this track is for businesses in the food and beverage industry. I'm going to learn a lot about growth and fundraising and what that looks like because our growth is at some point going to require a lot more cash to support the purchase orders and marketing. We've grown very slowly, very organically, but I think really smart, as well. We've been self funded and sustained this whole time, which is honestly really rare in this industry. And I think we know who we are and see the vision for the brand. It's definitely not the way most food brands grow.

Due to her health, my grandmother has had to step back. Working with your family changed our relationship a bit initially. It became much more of a business relationship for a couple of years, and we definitely had some tension at times. As the business has grown and we fell into our individual roles a little bit better, I feel like we learned how to be grandmother and granddaughter again. It's been really sweet that we found our stride after those first couple years, and she truly feels like my grandmother for sure and not just my business partner.

I do see myself exiting the business in some capacity in the next 10 years. I love being a mother, and I do want to be there for my girls as much as I can. Also, a big reason for wanting an exit at some point is that it's a lot of stress. It's a lot of responsibility. It's a totally different business now. I have a lot more meetings and calls and more traveling than I've ever had in the past. And so, I'll be ready for a time to be around when my girls more when they are young teenagers. We'll see...I say that, but it's hard for me to really not see RoRo's in my life in some capacity. So never say never!

At the time when we first started, I saw all the shiny things tied up with being an entrepreneur, and I thought that was appealing to me. I saw flexibility, as I wanted to be a mother. I wanted to be available. I do think that I'm getting there, but it took a long time. It's not an overnight thing by any means.

As I've gotten older and the business has grown, I've also realized that financial gain and business growth will never bring me true joy and will never fill a void in my life. I've realized that, you know, money is wonderful, but it's not going to make me happy. At the end of the day, my priority is my family. People will laugh that I'm on calls, and there will be a child screaming in the background. Or, I'll be in my car going to pick them up. And that's okay with me. I'm happy doing things in an unconventional way as a working mother. Learning not to compare to what everyone else is doing or how they are doing it has been really freeing for me. I think if we had raised a bunch of money right out of the gate, and grown super fast, we would have absolutely lost who we are as a brand. I wouldn't change a part of our story, and am so proud of how far we have come and that we are still here!

Chapter 4

George Seay

George Seay and his co-founder, Dan Asip, wanted to start a record label in Nashville. They were met with doubts from many industry veterans that you could successfully launch a record label in the modern market. But they were undeterred and set out to prove they had a business model for Acrophase Records that could work, founding their company while still living in their college dorms.

We saw a big gap between the artists signed to a major label and the artists that were developing and trying to start their careers with no backing, and no ability to properly distribute their music, whether digitally or physically. Historically, there was a huge barrier between major labels and their distribution networks and independent labels that prevented these smaller developing artists from getting discovered by consumers.

In 2017, the major labels were still learning how to reinvent themselves and distribute music through the new DSPs (digital streaming platforms), such as Spotify and Apple. The indie artists and indie labels were learning, as well. There was kind of a gap whereas an "independent label" entity, we were able to properly release albums and connect with the people at Spotify and Apple. But we had insight into how that would work and how we would build a company with the infrastructure to properly distribute these smaller artists. It was a time when the music industry was really starting to adapt to the new market where streaming was king. If we had not been starting in that time period, I don't think we would have been able to build the relationships with those distributors and those platforms like Spotify and Apple.

We got in, and we made these relationships with people that we still send new music to today. And now we have some notoriety and the ability to say we're Acrophase Records and people actually know what that is! We have the track record now. It was a unique time because it shifted so much from people finding new music in a record shop, on iTunes, or on a blog, to editors at Spotify and Apple and all the major streaming platforms creating editorial playlists for consumers to discover new songs. And we made connections with the editors of those playlists. They liked what we were putting out. And we built from there. We became almost like an A&R[4]

---

[4] Artists and repertoire (A&R) is the division of a record label that scouts and

directly to these platforms where they got new, fresh music from us. Dan and I were very picky about our curation. We picked the right song and the right artist that would connect with a broader audience. That can be a luck thing.

Something I preach to any up-and-coming artist we're trying to sign is that they need representation. They need someone to go out and speak for them and say, "This is great. I know it's great. Here's this artist." And these curators, all they do all day is listen to new music. If you're you're not presenting it to them in a concise, professional way and giving them a link to listen immediately, they'll probably keep sifting through their inbox and not even give it a chance. I think we brought a lot of professionalism to that pitch to them. We built a reputation with them after sending them hundreds of songs. The message gets across a lot more clearly from someone saying, "I'm a label, and I represent this artist," rather than an artist saying, "I represent myself, and here's my music. Will you give it a shot?" That is a very different pitch.

We see ourselves as partners in promoting these bands. We succeed when they succeed, which is why we start at a 50/50 split. We do recoup our big investments, like pressing vinyl records, which is very expensive. We would recoup that cost and then split 50/50 from there on any royalties past that point. Another big revenue stream is sync licensing. We have a partner that pushes songs to TV, movies, and advertisements.

We don't take master ownership of any work as a major label would. Once the term of our contract is over, they can walk away and take their master somewhere else, or we can renegotiate our deal. It's not often a loyal industry. Everyone's trying to get theirs, and it gets to be very cutthroat in certain situations, which we've seen multiple times. Our number one goal is to work with people that we enjoy being around. We have mutual victories together and celebrate those together. I think that's the most rewarding part of the industry and what I do.

My partner Dan and I lived together for the majority of the early years, which was definitely a stressor. We were in our early twenties, and one of us would be playing video games in the middle of a Wednesday afternoon while we were thinking about deadlines for an album at the same time. Or, you know, someone's cooking ramen in the kitchen, and we're talking about vinyl pressing deadlines, things like that. I was working other jobs at

---

develops new talent.

the time. It was an entrepreneurial venture that we were trying to go into, so don't expect a paycheck, and don't take a paycheck until you truly can. We didn't take a paycheck for a very long time, probably two years from when we were incorporated. Now it's become my full-time job. And I was very glad to quit my last job, a part-time thing I was doing on top of all this stuff.

Over the last three years, we've doubled revenues every year. But I wasn't entirely sure if that would be sustainable. I was way more nervous about taking a bigger paycheck. I was pulling back the reins and saying, "Let's wait just a little longer."

Now it's at a point where it feels very sustainable, and we're changing the way we format some deals. We're moving into a managerial role with some artists that are able to sign a bigger deal with another label. Things like that are happening, and it feels a lot more secure, which is a huge victory. It felt very, very good to quit that last job and feel secure and that our business would pay both of our paychecks and we'd be able to do all the things we want to do for these artists. A big goal, and something I tell every artist that we sign, is, "I want this to be your career. I want you to be able to tour and support yourself off your music because I think you're that talented." So. it was a victory for both of us to be able to support ourselves financially from our business and to have artists make it their career. We see it completely as a partnership, and it's a way for us to support music we really love and people we really love.

Our work relationship is unique in that in the early days, we were kind of competitive with each other because we were both attempting to go out and sign that next big artist. So, it was kind of funny, going back and forth, talking about the victories each of these artists had because we worked independently of each other on making certain decisions with these artists in each of our independent camps. But over the years, we both have identified strengths within each other. He's a really, really strong creative mind. He's an independent thinker and a really great networker. He meets a lot of people that have become partners of ours and helped our business grow. I'm a little bit more type A: organizational, accounting, the business structure of contracts, and legal negotiations. Over the past year and a half, that's become clearer. And I think we have structured roles that each of us are in command of. We're always working independently of each other and counterbalancing each other in a great way. From where we were at 19 trying to sign artists to a label, and now we're 27, we have a really big mutual appreciation for each of our strengths and aren't afraid now to reach out when there's an issue and work together to figure out how to solve it.

Since you started the business partnership, you've also started another partnership. You got married. How do you balance your two worlds?

My wife Reagan has been in my life since we started the label in our dorm room. She's seen it all happening and has always been a big supporter and believer in me. And I've never felt from her the stress of, "You're running your own business. What are we going to do if this collapses?" I've never felt that pressure from her. She's very supportive of me doing what I love and a job that I feel I'm really good at. We're living the "dual income no kids" life right now. She's a nurse, working on her own career, and I think that adds a level to the partnership. Now, it might not always be that way. She might stay home once we have kids, and then the financial burden is more on me to go out and make whatever amount of money we need to be comfortable. She loves Dan. She loves Dan's fiancée Gianna. We've all been friends for a long time now. He's getting married next year. I would say that my business and personal partnerships together are something that can be hard to balance. There are times when I'm stressed over work, and I may not want to share the things I'm stressed about with Reagan. Or maybe there are times when I'm working on something in my marriage and working on our relationship by taking time away from work.

But I would say having your own small business allows you that freedom to focus on different things happening at different times in life. And I don't have to call in sick to handle something with my family, which is a huge life benefit. I just can't state enough how great running your own small business is for your work/life balance and your ability to really focus on your personal relationships along with your business relationships.

I'll just add one more little tidbit. In my very, very short career, I haven't noticed many moments being huge moments, but rather a collection of small work put in over days and hours, and all of that built up to where it is now. I never saw a moment that was just like, "click," you've made it. It's a collection of a lot of things. And I think I had the misconception that there would be a "bang click" moment. But looking back now, it's just a string of thousands of things that get done. So, for me, if you're doing the work, if you're connecting with the right people, if you're putting yourself out there, things generally work out. That's how I feel. I'm a bit of an optimist that way. I just think you got to put yourself into the thousands of little things and the hundreds of thousands of hours, and it'll eventually work out. If you do that, you're an "overnight success"!

Chapter 5

Ryan Reisdorf

Ryan Reisdorf wanted to become a nurse, not because he had a lifelong yearning for that vocation, but because he is Type 1 Diabetic and wanted to learn more about the disease that had dominated his life growing up. His goal as a nursing student was to focus on prevention, not treatment. Once in nursing school, however, his passion shifted from nursing to addressing health and prevention issues as an entrepreneur.

The transition from being a nursing student to becoming a business owner came from my observations – in class, at clinical or even seeing industry trends in bustling Nashville, TN . I was looking for something that I loved and enjoyed and that could be directly related to our health. Sitting in nursing school in the heart of Nashville at Belmont University, I would look down Wedgewood[5]. There were 5,000 Airbnbs and two hundred bachelorette parties on any given weekend coming to this city. And they're staying in these beautiful homes. They were using the kitchen for beer, seltzers, frozen pizza, and not much else. And then I also saw that in Davidson County[6], there are 5,000 restaurants, from coffee shops to cafes to Michelin-star restaurants.

I just started pedaling around, asking questions out in the community, going to restaurants and asking, "Hey, could you guys come to my house tonight and make dinner, like your menu in my house? I'll pay you double what is being paid in the restaurant for the extra effort and time."

And they said, "No, we can't do that. That will never work. We would have to pull our workforce out. We just don't have that. It won't work."

I would then contact catering companies and ask if they are available in two weeks to make dinner for eight people. Two weeks went by, but I didn't hear from them.

We live in a world of automation and instantaneous gratification. Restaurants, catering companies, private chefs are not necessarily hitting that. And so that's where I saw a massive opportunity to create a pipeline that is automatic and fairly straightforward, which was incredibly

---

[5] Wedgewood Avenue is the main road bordering the campus of the university.
[6] Nashville is in Davidson County.

important.

I sat in class listening to cardiology lectures, diabetes lectures, and kidney failure lectures while I learned how to build and piece together the first Placemat website. I was copying the user experience of booking a hotel room, an Airbnb, a rental car, and I just replaced all of those elements with food. That vision was that this user experience is already out there, and people trust it a la Airbnb or Uber. They could rent a car in Los Angeles when they were in Nashville. They show up, and the car is there. That's a huge psychological experience that's been cracked by these companies. My target became to change the way that food is delivered and experienced in the comfort of your own home. I'm going to create this pipeline, and I'm going to create an opportunity for chefs, culinary talent, home cooks, and students to make money in a way that never existed before. Creating a brand-new job marketplace became another target – creating jobs out of thin air. I wanted to create jobs and an economy that essentially never existed. And I just kept working on it day in and day out. I'd rather build a website than write a report on what I would do during a clinical rotation. I knew my impact could be larger. I could either care for 5 chronically sick patients at a time at the hospital over the course of 12 hours or I could create and share a message in someone's home regarding the importance of our health with a feel-good food experience over the course of 3 hours. It was quite clear to me.

Probably for the first year or year and a half, I was just peddling these dinners. I would put my nursing clinicals and test schedule on the website as our "blackout dates." I was creating these boundaries to protect myself, but it also made us look busy. For example, I couldn't do every Friday because I often had a clinical from 6 a.m. to 4 p.m. I would manage the CRM[7] in the back of my nursing notebook.

My first customer was on a Friday afternoon. I went to Whole Foods and got two brown bags of groceries for 130 bucks. When I started this, I was a junior, and I made $39,000 in a semester of peddling dinners. And last year, we did $1.9 million.

Recently, I hired a consultant to help build some scalable systems to really build a strong, sturdy foundation so that we could go to Atlanta or Birmingham because there's a need and a demand there, like everywhere, but this was regional and within reach. This gentleman came from the

---

[7] Customer relationship management

restaurant industry. He was ten years my senior and had experience that I didn't have. When he came on, four people left. I care so much about people, because it's how Placemat generates revenue. I care so much about the culture that I created. I let the consultant run and do what he was hired to do, but it became catastrophic and damaging. I lost control of the company's foundation and why it all started and on what core philosophies. It was hard. I brought that baggage home to my girlfriend, and I could not let go of what this person was doing. It finally hit a wall, and I lost control of the most important piece of the company, its culture. I lost control of what felt like everything. And it was so lonely. This consultant didn't care about the most important piece of our puzzle, which was the workforce. I took back control. I took back the reins, which in hindsight to this day was one of the most valuable failures and lessons I've learned in regard to leadership and teamwork.

You got into this to try and improve people's health. Do you find any tension between what people want to eat and what they should eat?

I got connected with a gentleman through the Nashville Entrepreneurship Center. He's a contributor for the Wall Street Journal in The New York Times about the hotel industry. I pitched him on what I was doing. And he's like, "You've got it wrong, man. You're leading with something that 90% of the world doesn't care about – health. You're providing a seamless way for somebody to have a private chef come to their home. That's it. Nothing more, nothing less. When you get into the home, that's when you get to talk about health and the why of Placemat. When they take that first bite, that's when you get to talk about health. That's where your value is."

And sure enough, I took his advice and haven't looked back. It's changed the direction of the company.

Where is the business now, and where is it headed?

There was a need for a unique dining experience brought into your home that was different than catering. It is more hands-on. It is more personalized. We show up with the ingredients and whip up dinner. That's how we got started.

Second, we do the Placemat prepared meals that we deliver Monday through Friday. Whether you just want a meal taken off, so you don't have to cook, or you just had a baby, or you have type two diabetes, or you're going through chemotherapy, or you're a Titans player, or you're a

Predators player, we can deliver prepared meals.

The third one we do is corporate catering, using the same food setup but in offices.

And then the fourth one is our philanthropic wing. We take profits from the profit side of the business, and then we also collect private money from grants and private funds. We have specified demographics in the community who need food. We distribute this same healthy food that we're giving to the athletes and celebrities to homeless groups, ministries, metro students and individuals with chronic health issues. We're making an impact on the community from several directions.

COVID did things to everybody. On March 17th, I wrote a company-wide message that we were canceling all reservations because my health background kicked in and to be quite honest I was trying to remain in a place and make a decision that wouldn't get scrutinized or ridiculed. This is where we pivoted. We started with this great network of clients who wanted to do something. And so, a former Belmont alum Rene Ramirez, created the connections in the communities, with the ministries, the homeless, because there's a need especially during this time. We gave away our Placemat prepared meals. We started with one client and got up to 600 homes in a month.

Now we're in this unique position five years in. I've had private investors, institutional money, and VCs come to us. I'm holding out for the right fit. We've got the tiger by the tail, but I'm not going to sell out for money. I started with $130, and today we have just shy of $300,000 in capital.

In the next three years, we'll be looking for private investors, institutional investors, who believe in our vision of being a global company. The three-year plan is to have a bucket of investors who believe in our mission and in our values. We need the right partnership and the right people to enhance what we're pursuing.

Chapter 6

Tyler Bedwell

I first met Tyler and her husband, Adam (whose story is in another chapter), at my favorite local taproom. A random conversation at the corner of the bar left me excited to learn more about each of their entrepreneurial journeys. Tyler always knew she wanted to be in a creative field and eventually found her way into graphic design. After working in corporate settings, Tyler struck out on her own in what eventually became her business called Studio B Print and Design.

I took on some freelance work for friends and family members, basically doing a lot in the stationery world and wedding industry. I wasn't necessarily passionate about the work I was doing, but it was work. I had that mindset that I had to pay the bills. I kind of convinced myself that this is what you're supposed to do. Then, there was a major turning point when I realized that I love supporting small businesses—I always have since growing up in Maine. It seemed very natural to start helping other small businesses with their visual identity. It just sort of started.

At first, it was designing logos to full websites and everything in between. But now, I've narrowed it down to exclusively offer brand identity packages for passionate entrepreneurs and small businesses who value a modern-meets-classic aesthetic. It's very non-corporate. I work with everything from local restaurants and pubs, to boutique hotels and artisan coffee shops, to lifestyle photographers and creative entrepreneurs.

Even though I have a graphic design degree, I've been an artist for as long as I can remember, although I put that aside for years. I think just in my mindset, you know, culture convinces you that if you're an artist, you won't do anything. But I got to a point where I was like, "I can't *not* do it anymore." It sets my heart on fire more than *anything* else. And so, I started offering watercolor and pen commissions. I split the business to where it was both design *and* art. I did a lot of illustration work for my design clients anyway. There's something tangible about having a pen and paint, getting it on paper, and handing it to a client.

My grandmother was a Maine watercolorist. She was well known for her time and very traditional in her style and technique. There's a painting of hers of all the trees that grow in Maine, showcased at the state capitol. I was close to my grandmother, despite our very different personalities. But I think because I found interest in what she did, there was just that closeness and that bond there. She painted me ballet slippers when I was in high school because I was a ballet dancer for over 20 years in Maine. I have it hanging in my studio as a reminder. I have a piece of her with me in my studio every day, which is really, really cool.

She passed away when we were in college. I would hope she'd be proud of me now. It's been special keeping that legacy going, both through design and art. I love the idea of building a lasting legacy. I want to provide clients with a product that's going to last a lifetime. It's not just going to be a trend and pass. Whether it's commemorating a pet, a house, or a building, it is that 30 years from now, you still have it, and you can look at it just like I do with my grandmother's painting and say, "Oh, what a great memory!" I try to work with people who share that sentiment.

I really enjoy the creative life. I love to be able to work with my hands in that way. And so it was really neat that my design work segued me into finding art again. As much as I love designing, it's not exactly fulfilling. So, having that balance has been nice.

A lot of graphic designers are not necessarily fine artists. They're usually very much in the digital world. And that's fine. I mean, those people are very good at the corporate-type setting. I've gravitated more toward branding where it's integrating both worlds. My clients are very similar, kindred spirits, basically with lifestyle and aesthetic.

My business did not grow quickly. My husband, Adam, thankfully, fully supported what I was doing. It just grew from word of mouth. Someone saw the product I could provide for them, and then that person referred me to this person, and so on. It's been referral-based ever since the beginning. It wasn't really like some "aha moment" or anything.

A lot of the same people are customers on both sides of my business, too. I will do their small business branding, and then they'll commission a painting from me. From a marketing standpoint, you have to know who your people are. You have to know your target audience. I believe my potential clients gravitate towards my design and art style because they share the same core values, lifestyle, and aesthetic.

Thankfully, I'm at this point where I only book so many brand clients, leaving space for what I like to say is "booking myself" as the client. It gives me the space that I need in both time and mental space to focus on just painting. On Fridays, I try to be completely open to where I'm intentional about sitting down and painting, even if I don't feel inspired. A lot of artists wait for inspiration to get to them. And you can't do that. You can't. It's just not something that's feasible and practical. Once you start, you'll get into the groove. So, I just literally book "myself" on Fridays.

I work from home. I'm at the computer at 8:00, and unless there's a deadline, I try not to go past 5:00. I still treat it as if I were in "the office." I give myself an hour's lunch break in the middle of the day, and that's usually when I go to the gym to get my mind away from the house/office. Getting out of my office is important. There needs to be boundaries.

I design in my office. My walls are covered in things that inspire me, whether it's art or collected heirlooms. I think that it was very important for me to have a physical space that feels creative. The rest of the house can look neat and tidy. But this room is quirky. I could go for a larger room, but ultimately, it's been a very safe space to, you know, to be just who I am in my creative mind.

I paint in our bonus room area because of the natural light. It's more open and expansive than my office. The sun sets on that side of the house. It's very calming and gives me the mindset to just get into that headspace and gives me the physical space I need.

Where I'm at right now, it feels right. I've always had this mindset of significance over success. How can I do my part in this world and provide something that doesn't already exist? I'm trying not to fall into that comparison syndrome. Instead of focusing on success from what culture says is success, I'm focusing on a faith-based kingdom impact instead. And especially with social media, where it's so easy in what I do specifically to fall into that trap. I want to build my business and continue to grow so that I can then make a bigger impact.

God gave me the gift to create. And so, I feel that it's my purpose. It's taken me a long time to figure out that it's okay to put my work out there without feeling ashamed for some reason. Sadly, there's still a stigma around being an artist. I'm hopeful for the art side to continue to grow like the design side has. What I do physically requires my eyes to be good and my hands to be steady. And so, for the next 20 years, I have no intention of stopping—Lord willing.

With a deep-rooted foundation of faith, and led by the God-given call to create, I feel like it's my duty as Christian entrepreneur to share my work and the Good News with the world.

Chapter 7

Peter Smith

Peter Smith co-founded Golden Spiral Marketing with John and Bennett Farkas (father and son) when Peter and Bennett were finishing college. Like many startup marketing agencies, they took on various clients after launching. Over time, the agency pivoted into the niche of working with clients that are business-to-business healthcare tech companies. John and Bennett are creative types who fit well working in a marketing agency. Peter is a business generalist, which, as the agency grew, created professional challenges for someone with Peter's interests and skills.

Basically, I hadn't done anything else since we started this business when I was in college. I was not passionate about marketing. I fell into it. So that was weighing on me. I liked growing businesses. And the more I was learning about our business, and I don't want to sound arrogant, the more I was seeing that people who are more finance and business-driven don't gravitate toward small marketing agencies. I remember having a conversation with John where I was talking about how I was struggling to figure out exactly what I'm good at. What I'm good at is putting the pieces together. What I'm good at is creating a plan, mapping the plan, putting the right people in place, and helping them be successful in doing it. But marketing and client services were actually pretty draining for me. That was an identity crisis. That was weighing on me.

So, I actually gave John and Bennett my three-year notice. We had open communication. They knew I didn't love the business that we were in. I loved *running* a business. I loved the people I was working with. I liked what we were doing. But I wasn't finding fulfillment in what we were doing. And just honestly, I felt like I wasn't learning as much as I could because it was just a small marketing agency. I told them I wanted to figure out what my next thing might be.

I narrowed it down to three: private equity, venture capital, or becoming the CEO of a software company. My intention was to grow our business, get some people in that could fill some of my roles to where I could step out, and stay a partner. So, that was the plan. But it didn't happen. The business didn't grow. We didn't scale as quickly as I thought we were going to, and I didn't find the right people to put it in place.

I ended up talking with some fellow entrepreneurs with whom I had gone to college who were in different places. One had started a company that he wound down. The other had started a company that went extremely well. They had sold half of it to a private equity firm. He was interested in doing something on the side. He is a classic serial entrepreneur. We talked and ended up with the idea of an indoor putt-putt facility. We spent about nine months working together. We had built a whole financial model. We were sourcing the putt fields. We had put a letter of intent down on a space to rent. The other person and his brother, who had gotten involved with their private equity firm, had gotten to the point where they felt they needed to tell their peers that they were doing this. The private equity firm told them, "We see this is in conflict with your non-compete. You can't do it." They believed they could do it, but it wasn't worth the fight. It killed the idea, which was great because we were targeting a March 2020 launch, and we undoubtedly would have gone under due to COVID.

I had some friends that were going to start a daycare. I was going to invest in that and run the finance. The pandemic killed that as well. But what was really good about it was that it showed me that I wasn't necessarily unhappy with what I was doing. It was that I wanted to scratch some other itches, as well.

At about that same time, I got involved with a nonprofit, open-source software project focused on privacy-enhancing technologies. The goal is to open up the world's data. Right now, data is locked down in institutions or in Census Bureaus. The mission is to build software tools that allow you to do third-party research or data science without having direct access to data. That organization was getting a lot of momentum. I got involved on a volunteer basis. As I got in there, I quickly gravitated to what I'm better at. They needed a strategic plan to guide the organization. I created an agenda for that and got it off the ground. I became head of finance, helping with contracts and some of the partnerships. Bennett, my business partner, also serves as the head of brand. The organization is publicly partnered with the White House, New Zealand, the U.N. Privacy Council, Facebook, Twitter, and Microsoft.

So basically, this did two things. First, there was a philanthropy itch that I wanted to scratch. I wanted to do something as a volunteer. And second, it was the whole thing I was feeling that the stakes weren't very big in my company. Well, *these* stakes are about as big as they get! It was the biggest institutions in the world that were partnered to solve what I had learned was a really big problem. A lot of data is trapped and can't be used. We have so much data in the world, but we are limited in its use. So, the ability to open that up is a really exciting problem.

What that ended up doing was making me very happy with my current job. I have a situation where I'm able to do both at the same time. My partners are very gracious and let me spend as much time as I need volunteering there, so long as I get all my stuff done.

I still have the same ambition and hope for our business. I love the company. I mean, I really do. And part of my re-engagement in it has been I don't feel that I've accomplished enough with it. It's not as big or successful as I believe it can be. And you know what? When I talked about what I was interested in doing, I eventually circled back to the fact that I'm basically a "private equity guy." That's just kind of my DNA. I'm more geared toward that. I am interested in continuing to start or buy pretty standard businesses. My current one, it's a traditional service model. I know how to do that. I believe Golden Spiral will be a wonderful portfolio company for me. That's kind of how I see it. I still intend to transition out at some point and perhaps just oversee the finance side.

What I've learned is that I'm really good at building a culture. I think it all comes down to our values. We built a really good system for hiring people based on those values. I've focused on what it means to build a scalable culture and a scalable business. If I'm going to go do this with other companies, well, I have to do it at mine first. The thing that's been reinvigorating is that I don't feel that I've really scaled our business to the degree that we can.

Adapting to the pandemic was a surprisingly easy transition since we have been very deliberate about our company values. Our values aren't just something we said once and then pointed to them when there was an H.R. issue. We do two evaluations a year with a rubric. Each person evaluates themselves, and the manager evaluates them on how well they're embodying the values. We also do an anonymous company survey twice a year. Each person goes line by line and grades how well the company embodies the value. We've added a hiring tool, which we call our "hiring alignment." Before we post the job, we map out all the attributes and traits that someone needs in this role. We want people from different backgrounds to be additive to our company. But there still has to be DNA alignment with our values. So, what that did was help us evaluate candidates objectively based on how well they embody the traits, attributes, and values.

So, when we went remote during the pandemic, we did pick up on some different traits and attributes of people that weren't as effective in that environment. If we're going to be remote, we need people that are all pretty independent.

Candor is our most important value. When we do the onboarding and take people through the values, I always tell them I'd like them to feel comfortable performing candor. We need to show them that they're not going to be reprimanded for that candor. We believe it takes some time for people to really feel comfortable doing it. I do think it's an area where once it's there, our culture is contagious. We have enough people who have been here a long time who just embody it really, really well.

I'd say one key thing we're doing since we've gone remote is in-person retreats every six months. Each of them has been two days. We bring people into town and get hotels or Airbnbs. We do about a 90-minute working session, and everything else has been fun. We do a meal with everyone. This last one, we did this thing called "the chef and I," where they give you a bunch of ingredients and cook together. It's a kind of team-building type of stuff. We've also done Topgolf and gone bowling. It's highly focused on just spending time together. It's gone really, really well. A couple of people no longer fit the culture that did leave. And it was the right thing. We've been hypersensitive to who we've hired since then.

Chapter 8

Mark Rubenstein

Mark Rubenstein's background was in hospitality, food, and beverage. He attended the Culinary Institute of America and gained valuable experience to work in restaurants. After graduation, he became a corporate chef and trainer for a big restaurant brand where he worked for several years and was able to learn the business side of running a successful operation. He eventually opened his own place, and then moved into owning a consulting business that helps restaurant and bar owners improve profits. This is where he developed the relationships that led to the opportunity to co-found A Head For Profits, which got its start as a business that cleaned draft beer lines in bars and restaurants.

The beer distribution industry is governed by what they refer to as a three-tier system, which was created after the repeal of prohibition. The wholesalers, the suppliers, and the retailers are independent, but they must work together. From being in the restaurant business and consulting with many in the industry, we knew that the industry was going to explode with the advent of craft beer. Lipman Brothers[8] asked the founders of A Head for Profits to put a business model together that meets the operational guidelines that suppliers demand of them by contract. And part of that is maintaining the integrity of the beer line. As the craft beer movement grew, the distributors looked to outsource this segment of their responsibility and preferred to focus on marketing and distribution. A Head for Profits spent six months on business planning resulting in a contract for 500 beer lines at a great price. We went to market with a handful of employees and today we manage more than 120,000 beer lines and more than 300 employees.

There were three founders of A Head For Profits: myself, Mark Davis, and Jeff Walton, who all have hospitality backgrounds. We are now a partnership of six representing all three tiers from the Beverage Distribution Industry.

Believe it or not, you don't really know what's out there until you get out there. You could go to Broadway Brewhouse, where they have 92 taps, and nobody really knows which supplier was responsible for which of the taps. If you talk to a retailer, they refer to that as real estate because there is a value to that tap, as they're putting a premium product on it. They sell it

---

[8] One of the largest beverage distribution companies in Tennessee.

for a certain markup, and they know what's on the tap. But the wholesalers and the suppliers have no idea what's on there. For us to even be able to clean just Lipman lines, and not for the other distributors in town, took a lot of feet on the street. Literally we started by getting out there with a pad and paper to figure out exactly whose lines were whose.

It was very manual -- all pen and paper. There was no technology. There was no third-party software that we could employ. Part of the opportunity for us was that distributors really didn't know where they had their tap real estate. They relied on their sales teams out on the street to tell them what was there. But the sales force didn't always tell their bosses where they were winning taps in their market.

We were going from restaurant to restaurant, coming back, working with Lipman, and telling them what we found. But we also had to engage at a retail level, letting them know what we were doing. Now restaurants have a third-party company coming in. We had to reorient each and every retail establishment because we were servicing their systems. It's their product that we're dispatching to clean the lines. So, it's building a relationship client by client and communicating with Lipman what we're doing. Most importantly, we were able to educate the bar owners regularly on why clean beer lines matter so much to taste and, most importantly, to their bottom lines.

A Head for Profits is a route-based business model. We encountered routing challenges as our business grew, as you can only get into bars at a certain time before they open. If you think about Broadway[9] here in Nashville, all the bars close late. They have teams coming in as early as 7 a.m. and open the doors at 11 a.m. You have a narrow window during which you can provide your services.

Recently, the sexiness of craft beer has waned to some extent. We think the beer industry as a whole is losing market share to spirits and wines. You're seeing the high-end crafts lose market share internally to the traditional light lagers of the world. And at the same time, we're still seeing growth in breweries. Roughly 200 brands enter the market daily. Not necessarily craft brewers but brands within crafts breweries that are being introduced. So, it's volatile.

As we see adult beverage consumption swapping within the liquor, beer

---

[9] The Honkytonk district in Nashville, TN.

and wine categories, A Head for Profits has been diversifying to include all beverage dispense systems. So we are now selling, installing, repairing and maintaining all equipment systems such as wine and cocktails on tap, Nitro cold brew, we don't really care what people drink. We just want to be able to dispense it all and manage it all. We now service wine and cocktail lines. The industry is diversifying. We're working on incremental revenue per bar that we service regularly.

And COVID also impacted the industry. We are seeing more automation, fewer humans touching stuff, and more technology promoting dispense because it's healthier for the retailer. The industry got crushed in human resources during COVID. We think fine dining will certainly be the way it's always been, but the average retailer is now going to use technology where they wouldn't have even considered it before. We're seeing it now.

We provide great transparency and are beginning to work with other businesses, such as point-of-sale companies. As stated, we see automation will have a significant role in the hospitality industry moving forward. Over the last ten years, we've invested heavily in our own performance software. It's all built into our apps. We not only know where the beer placement is, but we know how beer is sold, the time of day it's sold, its price points, and its menu mix compared to other products. And so, we are in a market share game now. We want to clean lines, sell systems, and maintain those systems.

Market share is especially valuable for data. Part of our growth strategy will be to move into the major markets. Today we service around 80 wholesalers. We clean about 110,000 beer lines. We touch roughly 22,000 restaurants on a regularly scheduled basis in 13 contiguous states. We came into this wanting to consolidate the industry. We want to control 40% of the available market as far as retail locations because data is more and more valuable to both our customers and to us.

For the first many years we focused on organic growth, expanding our existing client base in the primary region of the Southeastern and Middle Atlantic states with one round of private equity to help us scale. The next rounds of funding will be to accelerate acquisitions. The beverage dispense service industry within all three tiers has historically been fragmented. We have always seen this as the opportunity for our growth. We have acquired businesses in Illinois and California and are looking for more in major markets that we can move into.

One of the best days in our company history was buying Glacier Design Systems in California because that was a company we knew about. For us to accelerate to a point where we could buy them was quite satisfying. Mark Davis and I flew into LA on a Tuesday evening. We sat in a neighborhood park about three-quarters of a mile away from the facility until shortly after 5:00. We then drove over there and met with the owner and a business broker for approximately fifteen minutes. I think they just wanted to make sure we were for real.

We closed that deal in April. Several of us met with the owner the evening before the closing. He told us that nobody in their team knew about the sale other than the two people in the room. The next morning, he put us in front of his eighteen employees. And he literally said, "I just sold the company, and here are the new owners." And he walked out of the room. I'm not typically speechless, but I really had to think carefully about what to say.

Several employees were quite alarmed and anxious. We currently employ everyone except two people who culturally didn't fit. Some of those people now have much broader leadership roles, and two have relocated to our home offices to take on bigger roles. I did not like what happened in our Glacier sale because I don't think it's fair to the employee.

The next sale initiated when I caught wind that Stuever and Sons[10] were going to close their doors. The father was aging out. The family dynamic was that the youngest son was running it but he didn't want to anymore. I called them and said, "Are you guys selling, or are you just closing the doors?" And the son said, "Yeah, but I think we have somebody internally we might sell it to, and I think you're too late". I said, just give me 5 minutes.

A half-hour later, he and his father called and said, "We'd much rather talk to you than who we were already talking to."

Mark Davis and I flew up two days later and met with them. At that point, though, all their employees believed that the business was shutting down. It took 90 days from start to finish to close on that deal. The reason we got it, and we got it for the price we did, was because we were willing to do it that fast. It was a little bit sloppy. Our many, many visits we were literally ingratiating ourselves to the employee community just to keep the staff.

---

[10] Located in Chicago, IL

They are really knowledgeable and were worth the extra effort to keep them.

Currently, we have four other NDAs[11] out now for potential acquisitions, two of which will accelerate in quarter one. And in both of those, once we do get a letter of intent, we will be much more disciplined on the rules of engagement as to how we actually execute this stuff. I'm not an M&A guy. I know this industry. But some of the other stuff I've had to learn as we go.

I am a firm believer in over communicating to our staff. The more they know about what's going on, the more they are able to focus efforts on what is important to the company and understand why their role is an important one.

---

[11] Non-Disclosure Agreement

JEFFREY CORNWALL

SECTION 2

PERSEVERANCE WHILE DANCING WITH THE MARKET

"Many of life's failures are people who did not realize how close they were to success when they gave up."
Thomas Edison

Chapter 9

Tyler King

Tyler King grew up in St. Louis. His first job was as a server in a restaurant, and he has continued to work in the food service industry ever since. When he went away to college, he got a job working for the food service vendor at the university. By his sophomore year, Tyler had been given management responsibilities. He continued to work in the restaurant industry after graduating from college. The long hours typical in food service work led Tyler to decide that if he was going to work that hard, he might as well do it for himself. So, Tyler launched Tastify to take advantage of the growing trends in the personal chef segment of the industry. Like many entrepreneurs, he worked a day job to help support his personal chef and catering business get launched.

A typical day when I first got started was really busy. I woke up at about 5:00 in the morning and was going to work. I was cooking for the university. It was a cushy corporate job that I hated, but there were benefits, it seemed like pretty reasonable pay for a cook, and they were very flexible if I needed a week off on short notice for a big catering job. Depending on the day, I'd usually be off at about 3:00 or 4:00. Then I'd run home, prep, and go to sleep. Then, I'd wake up the next day and go to work until 3:00 or 4:00. I'd grab all that prep and load it in a cooler, go to the event and get to work.

I was in a lot of pain. I was working every day, and I had a herniated disc in my back. I had pain radiating down my leg and I hadn't gotten much of a break in my business. I was working really hard for just a few bucks. If I could go out and cater an event, make a hundred bucks, and dump 8 hours of my day into it, I was doing that. My day job was paying for it.

I got a call from this girl named Annie, that I met at a friend's wedding. She was the wedding planner. She was sitting in the back of the room and was the only one not dressed up. And she had her hair in a bun and was working on her computer at the wedding. I just went up and introduced myself as a guy who had just started a catering company and was willing to do whatever it took to get some work. I hadn't heard from her for a few months. Then all of a sudden, she gives me a call, and she says, "Hey, Tyler. I don't know if you remember me, but my name is Annie, and we met at this wedding. Well, I have a really big client, Amazon, and they want to feed their warehouse workers at one of their warehouses in Nashville the week of Thanksgiving. We're looking at about 2,000 people over three days."

She had my interest a little bit. And I thought, "No way. I'm not a catering company. I'm just a single guy with no team."

And she said, "I got a quote from another catering company. They came in around 60 grand and that's a little bit over budget."

I asked her where she needed to be. She said, "$30,000."

I said, "Let me let me go back to my end, and I'll get back to you as soon as possible."

The first person I called was my dad. I told him that I had to take this. He agreed and said to do it by whatever means necessary.

I was working out of my one-bedroom apartment. The kitchen was about the size of most bathrooms. So, I started to reach out to food trucks because food trucks typically are members of commercial kitchen spaces. I reached out to about 20 or 30 of them. And one guy reached back out to me and he said that I could use his kitchen.

He said, "Here's how much I'm going to want to make off this. I'll help you and my team is available to you. If anybody asks at the kitchen, you're working for me. But I understand that you're the boss here. I'll work for you, and we'll handle all the shopping. We'll partner up.

So, I ran the numbers. We came in around $38,000. We got the deal.

We had done an event six months earlier that paid out pretty decently. I think I made maybe $4,000 that I hadn't spent yet. I was just sitting on it. That $4,000 got me most of what I needed for the first day. The first day came to an end, and I was out of money. And so, I started racking it up on my personal credit card with all the other expenses for the rest of the week. By Wednesday, the day before Thanksgiving, it was about $20,000 in expenses.

I got a check for around 38 grand. It was the biggest check I had ever seen in my life. I remember sitting in my car, staring at this check. I almost didn't even want to cash it. I wanted to hold on to this check forever. That was one of the best days. I had an hour break between meal periods that we were serving these folks. I ran over to the Regions Bank, I sat down, and I handed the check over. I remember the guy's face was like, "Oh, wow!" My hand was shaking as I handed him the check. I was so nervous because I thought, "God, anything could go wrong." But I needed it deposited in my account. He said the funds would be available in 24 hours. I jumped out of that seat. I was so excited. We ended up making about ten grand in profit. That was the thing that fueled us.

I had to get back surgery a few months later. I sat on the 10 grand, and that's what got me through the back surgery and recovery and paying all those employees to do all those gigs. That was the best day of my entire life because I finally felt like, okay, now we have a little cushion. At the time, I didn't know I was going to have back surgery, but I thought, "We're going to make it." I can live on this for a long time because we were breaking even. We just needed a little reserve. We pulled off the Amazon event beautifully.

After I had gotten through back surgery, I had scheduled a wedding for 150 people. It was going to be at the 30-day mark after surgery. I'd be useful, but I needed to delegate a lot of tasks. But a few weeks after surgery, I got infected. It was pretty serious stuff. My surgeon instructed me to go straight to the hospital because I was vomiting. That's how I found out that I had a staph infection.

It was about four days until the event. I had people that had been working for me, but nobody that really seemed to stand out except for this one girl that had worked about five events with me, who just seemed to really care. I gave her a call. It was funny. This girl and I actually used to date. We had stopped dating, and she reached out to me a few months later and said, "Hey, I need a job. I know that things didn't work, but I need a job."

So, I gave her a call and said, "Hey, so this is going to sound kind of crazy, but I have to go back in and go back under and have the staph infection cleaned out. And I'm going to be on very, very heavy antibiotics for the next few days that are going to make me very sick. And we have a wedding for 150 people this weekend. I have some of the food orders in. I know you've never been to this venue, I know you've never met half my employees, and I know you've never met this client, but I need you to handle this for me."

And she says, "Okay. Let's talk about what you need."

I sat down at my computer and typed out as much as I possibly could, as many details as possible, in a short amount of time. I gave the time that she should arrive, the time that they were eating, all of the employees, and all their contact information. I started a group chat. I got in all the food orders that I possibly could, but she had to run to Costco and get a bunch of stuff. I created the shopping list and the prep lists. I got it right down to the very minute about what she should be doing and how. And I said I'll be available somewhat over the phone. It was a very cool, unique event. I was lying in a hospital bed post-surgery under strong antibiotics. That night, I probably got thirty phone calls from her. "Hey, we got the grill up and running, and it's not heating up." I mean, everything that could go wrong did. But they pulled off the event beautifully. She ended up killing it! She ended up being my best employee ever. She just had her heart in it, and she wanted to learn how to cook better and to manage people.

I realized that maybe it was time to prepare for this and to get people in the right places so that I'm never in this position again. It was a hard lesson.

A typical day today for me is quite different than it was in the beginning. I still wake up fairly early, but not as early as I used to. I exercise. Exercise is a big thing that I missed. Those couple of back surgeries in 2021 coming out of COVID, were really hard as a business owner. So, I decided that exercise had to become a priority for me if I was going to continue to be successful as a businessman. I need to be healthy because health issues are a distraction. I'm usually done exercising by 9:30 or 10:00. If it's an event day, I usually prep. I'll go to my event that night. I have an assistant who handles a lot of our bookings. She's very, very good at her job. My clients love working with somebody that's always available to answer an email or answer a phone call. If I don't have an event, I'm out there trying to get work. I'm networking, and setting up meetings. To me, it's about getting so much business that I'm stressed out and then having that consistently so we can grow and hire more people. That's growth for me.

Chapter 10

Shawn Glinter

Shawn Glinter is a successful serial entrepreneur currently working on a healthcare company called Pendant Biosciences.

Around 2002, I read a really cool article in *Popular Science* about how nanomedicine is going to transform the world. I didn't have a Ph.D. in engineering and science, and I didn't have to have any experience in nanotechnology. But I was really intrigued. And I've always been kind of a nerd and always loved science. So I figured I could go ahead and find a bunch of brilliant scientists, and we'd raise some money, start a company, and build something cool. But I live in the city of Nashville. We don't invest in biotech and in pharma here, especially in 2002. This is just a heavily services and delivery town when it comes to healthcare. I went to talk to about thirty really, really wealthy individuals, all white-haired dudes. But they said, "Shawn, we don't invest in this kind of stuff. Go do something in health care services. If you can sell it to a hospital, and a hospital will buy it, I'll invest in you."

It was a good idea that I listened to those individuals because hundreds of millions of dollars have gone into nanomedicine and nanotechnology from about 2002 to about 2009, and not a lot have been really successful.

It was 2010, and I had exited from a company and wanted to take a little bit of time off. I decided I wanted to go back and look at nanotechnology. I took a team of ten PhDs with various scientific and engineering backgrounds and a couple of MDs. I said, "Let's go find out what the latest and greatest in nanotechnology and nanomedicine is." You ask a Ph.D. for two ideas, and they bring you ten. It was pretty daunting to have this list of two dozen plus ideas for diagnostics, therapeutics, and devices.

A couple of guys in town said, "Hey, there are a couple of guys that have good biotech backgrounds. They could potentially also be good partners of yours. They've never really started companies, but they're solid, smart scientists."

We got together and took a look at the list of ideas. We narrowed it down to not wanting to do something that was going to be a "one trick pony" or something that was just going to be a single asset or a drug that we would have to bet the farm on. I was looking for something more platform-focused that would allow us to take a lot of shots.

We drilled down to thinking about how to deliver drugs in a safer, less toxic, more effective way over longer periods of time. Who wants to take pills three times a day or have to take shots multiple times a week? I got really intrigued by developing long-acting therapies and formulations for controlled and extended-release.

And the funny thing about that is some of this came to fruition when thinking about Viagra. We started looking at some of those drugs that were coming off patent. We were thinking about how we could not only create better formulations for drugs being delivered but in a way which you could extend the patent for another seventeen years. There was a good business case there, as well.

We narrowed it down that we were going to do something around nanotechnology for developing formulations for better therapeutic drug delivery. Since it would be hard to raise money to do this ourselves in a lab, we looked at universities that had researchers doing stuff in drug delivery. And it came down to Vanderbilt, MIT, and Princeton. We didn't like the technology from either MIT or Princeton. We wanted something that was disruptive and was going to be different.

We launched Pendant in 2012, but for the first two years, we were just we were kind of tinkering and trying to figure out some stuff. We were doing some things in the lab, but it wasn't really anything meaningful. I put in a couple of hundred thousand dollars of my own money in. We had others who had invested in previous startups of mine put in a couple hundred thousand dollars, so we had about $700,000 right out of the gate. Just to do some early chemistry. Towards the end of 2014, I realized we would have to raise some money, and I knew that we would not be able to get by on hundreds of thousands of dollars. Some would even say we should go out and raise maybe tens of millions of dollars and move to a city like Boston. It seems kind of strange to say that we bootstrapped a biotech company, but we bootstrapped a biotech company even though we've raised almost eight and a half million dollars, which is not chump change. But for biotech, it *is* chump change compared to what some of these other companies in San Diego, San Francisco, Houston, and Boston raise.

I got a call that asked me to apply to the Johnson & Johnson JLABS incubator. We got asked to apply to the JLABS incubator up in Toronto because our academic partner was up there. Rather than raising $8-10 million which almost half goes for bricks and mortar, now we were accepted to JLAB incubator in Toronto. With that, I have physical space, equipment, and instruments. All I need is super bright and talented scientists.

We had to decide if we were going to become a product-focused company or if we were going to become more of a material science or formulation-type company. By this time, we had moved away from nanotechnology. We started to focus on the novel materials of formulation science and developing long-acting therapies. And the delivery of long-acting therapies is not just nano: it's nano, micro, or even larger types of shapes and sizes. If we were going to focus on finding the right delivery device or delivery system it wasn't only going to be around "nano."

There was interest in Pendant's materials. The whole idea behind what we do is we use novel polymer materials to help develop a formulation that will deliver a drug better, sometimes over longer periods of time and smaller frequency. As the polymer matrix basically breaks down, it releases the drug. But we had to make the decision to not be a product company anymore and to become a material science company, which across the board, nobody really finds very sexy. They just don't. So that sucks, too, because I'm no longer in control. Now, I was relying on Big Pharma. I had to go out and sell our technology and gain interest among Big Pharma. When pharma gets excited about something, it's a herd mentality. But I mean, they're slow….very slow. We'd had so many calls with pharma, and they were intrigued. They'd be like, "This is really cool." Well, cool doesn't generate revenue for me". I mean, you can talk about how cool this technology is all day long. It took us years to really foster relationships with pharma.

Everybody thinks that when you've done all this work in the lab at your academic institution, you run these experiments, you generate data, and the data looks good, now we can go sell it and put this into humans. Well, that's the furthest from the truth. So much happens, so many things go wrong, and so many things can break down. Just the ability to take it from one academic lab and reproduce it in another academic lab in two separate institutions can be challenging. And now you're trying to go to a commercial lab where it's a little more structured and rigid. You're not talking about any kind of scale-up.

We knew that there would always be inherent challenges when you go from your academic lab, even to a small commercial scale, never mind a bigger commercial scale. I mean, everybody knows that. But there are so many variables to take into account. And so we went to a contract manufacturer that dealt with polymers. We said, "Listen, we need some kind of commercial help."

We determined some challenges were even bigger than we had anticipated. We were sitting here wondering do we go ahead? Is this what they call an "Old Yeller moment"? There are times when you just sit there, and it feels dark, and you're depressed and upset. Sometimes you're just so pissed off and angry. And sometimes I don't know that I have the right answer. Am I the guy that can get us through this? Will I get us through this? Should I cut my losses? And we had not only days and weeks, but we had months and months of this, just getting harder and harder.

And my guys were looking to me, even though they're the scientists because I'm the business guy. And I'm like, "You guys are the scientists! Go figure out the science!" But they're like, "No, you need to go figure it out!" There was a lot of tension because we just couldn't get the technology to reproduce in a way that was meaningful. I was trying to create a good story around the technology because we were going to have to go raise more money. I mean, you can't tell investors, well, this is really shitty technology. Trust me, we're going to make it work.

So what turned the corner? I would tell you that a lot of luck and a lot of perseverance. A lot of creativity. A lot of leadership. If the underlying science was good, and we just needed some time to figure it out, my team needed to know that we were going to be okay. I'm a grinder and a fighter. My guys would feed off me, and I would feed off of them. I told my guys, "You guys are smart. Let's just go ahead and just take baby steps, as hard as it is. We don't have to hit a home run right now. Let's try to figure out if we can re-engineer things to see if this will work. But we don't have to have it all figured out tomorrow. I'll make sure that the resources are there for us to do it." And I did.

But we got through it. At ten years old, we're in the best place we've ever been. We have 2 really significant pharma partners that are the furthest along with us. With one of them, we're two years or less from our first dosing into humans. We've done some pretty significant work in scaling up our materials.

There are only a couple of places around the world that specialize in manufacturing these kinds of materials. We had a domestic partner who had an operation in China. Because of COVID, we realized that we had a bad partnership with our contract manufacturer. Things just came to a head for us, which was going to be another very painful thing because we had spent hundreds of thousands of dollars with this one manufacturer. We don't have unlimited resources to create three or four redundant manufacturing processes. The other challenge is I don't want to share my secret sauce with three different manufacturers. We had to make a decision and hit the reset button. And that meant spending more money. There are times when it's just scary because you're not sure you're making the right decision. But I had to make a decision here. Half of my team supported moving to a new manufacturer, and the others were not. I said, "Okay, we're going to hit the reset button." But I can't just hand you a piece of paper with a protocol and a recipe and say to a new manufacturer, "Just go do this." You still have to let them create their internal processes. But here we are now. We're two or three weeks away from producing our first significant commercial batch.

I think my investors would love to see an exit on the horizon. Probably, I think, in twelve to eighteen months. They would be ecstatic to just see an exit. But at the same time, based on everything going on with this company and our trajectory, we should be ready to exit in the next three to four years.

I have had my fair share of founder fatigue that has ebbed and flowed over the last twelve to twenty-four months. There are just days when I'm just worn out because I'm tired of getting beaten up. I drive through it, but it doesn't mean I enjoy getting beat up or dealing with bullshit and stupidity.

But now, I've got this great team that is texting me on a Saturday evening! Things are good, and we've got really good commercial terms with these Big Pharma partners. My guys are excited about the science and the data that they're generating in our lab. My guys are jacked up right now. That's cool. They're excited.

You know, it's funny. People ask me, "Shawn, what are you going to do after you sell Pendant?" I will smoke a really good cigar. Drink a couple of glasses of a 25-year-old single malt scotch. I honestly try not to think about it. I try not to think about what's it like after Pendant for me. Whatever I do, I will probably do something that continues to be impactful on people's lives. Because, at the core, I think that's kind of how I'm wired. But I don't know. I really don't.

Chapter 11

Patrick Linton

Patrick Linton is an American who grew up in Asia, first in Japan and later Singapore. He moved to the U.S. to pursue a university degree in International Business and Chinese. After graduating, Patrick began his career with a large international consulting firm in San Francisco. He knew he always wanted to go back to Asia to work and live, so when the opportunity came, he transferred to the consulting firm's Singapore and then eventually the Tokyo office. While there, Patrick identified a need in the market not being met by any of the larger consulting firms. Eventually, he left his consulting firm and launched his own business, Bolton Remote, which helps fast-growing software companies build outsourced customer success teams.

I look back and think, wow, I had no idea what I was doing. I had a lot of confidence that I had a good product that was in the talent market. I knew that big companies like Accenture and IBM were leveraging outsourced talent in locations around the world. They were charging rates with huge profit margins built in. I wondered why small businesses weren't doing the same thing as the big guys in terms of building global teams. What's happening with the rest of the businesses that are not the big Fortune 1000 companies?

I discovered that at the time, small businesses were bringing on global talent, but it was through online staffing platforms. They were going to freelancer marketplaces like oDesk (which is now Upwork) and trying to get freelancers all around the world to do work for them. If they were experiencing a talent crunch in Sydney, San Francisco, New York, or wherever, they would go online and find somebody in Pakistan or the Philippines to fill that need. And they would try to get work done in a cost-effective way. What I found out is that just because they had access didn't mean that they actually knew what they were doing, or that they actually knew how to bring on somebody from a different country and culture remotely and properly integrate them into their businesses.

Our idea was to carve out a piece of a freelancer platform and do it better than the freelancer platform - we'd do it as a subscription service – "talent-as-a-service." We originally pitched ourselves as an alternative to oDesk. The U.S. market was a little bit saturated when it came to offshore outsourcers, but quickly realized that Australia was about five years behind the U.S. market when it came to leveraging global, remote talent. And if you look at the GDP of Australia at that time, it was the same GDP as Texas. The population is about the same as Florida. So, it was a great micro market to look at to start the business. I jumped on a plane, flew down to Sydney, and hopped across Australian cities, almost door-to-door, selling this idea – what we were calling "remote staffing" - to small businesses in Australia. And it worked. We started building a business with Australian companies.

I remember having dinner with a guy in Melbourne. He ran a $7 million-a-year manufacturing company. He was nearing retirement age, and he was going to have his son take over soon. We went out for dinner, and I pitched him on what we do. I think he was wondering why I was there. I didn't really have product/market fit yet, and my definition of the target market being "small businesses" was way too broad. I think he felt bad for me and paid for the steaks. He did end up paying us for one remote staff to do some NetSuite administration work. The deal that we sold him didn't even pay for my trip to Melbourne. But I learned a lot about small businesses and what types there were out there. After a career in consulting working with the world's biggest companies, I didn't really understand that world. I discovered professional services firms, consulting firms, manufacturers, brick-and-mortar stores, and all sorts of agencies. I started to really understand the landscape of what we consider to be a "small business" and where the real potential markets were.

My team and I then started looking at different small business markets. After accumulating a number of customers in the Australian market, we sold to a small company out of Mountain View, California, which was just another small business to us. It was actually a venture-backed tech company. They called us up after they raised $65 million and said, "We need to grow a team of 30 people with you guys. Can you do it 24/7? Can you build this type of capability?"

I said, "Yeah! Yeah, we can do that!"

And they said, "Good because we're coming to Manila." They jumped on a plane, and we started building a team together.

I said, "This is the kind of business we should be in. We should be helping these hypergrowth 'small businesses.'" That was around 2014 when we were only a year old, and tech just boomed in the following years.

That led to a complete change in our strategy and focus. It is an interesting market. These businesses were raising a lot of money. They needed to grow fast. The big outsourcing players out there wouldn't touch these guys, and frankly they didn't know how to even work with them. A lot of venture-backed companies were using freelancer platforms to patch together some kind of a solution. The founders were really smart young guys who were digital savvy and digital natives. But when you get fourteen or fifteen freelancers from across the world, and you're trying to coordinate some kind of an operation, and you're trying to grow, it really is very inefficient – freelancer churn is a huge problem, but also doing things like continuous process improvement, quality control, and risk management. These were all nearly impossible bringing on freelancers through these platforms.

When we talked to these businesses, they said, "Great. Cost savings. That's a given. We know in a global world, we're going to get cost savings. Can you scale? How fast can you guys go? If we need 30 people next week, and we didn't plan for it, can you do that?"

A lot of times in these scaling tech companies these guys are not doing resource planning. And so, our answer just became, "Yes!" And we started selling scalability.

We just started learning more and more about these companies and started really getting inside of them. We ended up designing a service that was appropriate for companies that are post-Series A but not as good for pre-Series A – and we knew why and how to coach them through their talent options. We started understanding the types of services that made the most sense to deliver, and when they made sense. And luckily, with the venture dollars flowing into these companies increasing every single year, we realized we could start to specialize. There were enough companies out there to work with – the total addressable market was growing. And so, we ended up specializing in very specific services and even specializing in the type of venture-backed company we worked with. We ended up honing our core services to be perfect for B2B Software-as-a-service (SaaS) companies, mostly later stage, but still private. I would say our strategy was honed by the market. We just listened constantly at every customer touchpoint. My team and I were constantly listening to customers and asking questions, sharing what we learned at other similar firms, connecting people. We started focusing on how to build the right experience for an individual working in our customer's business. Instead of focusing on Company X, which just raised its series B, what about focusing on the V.P. of Customer Success in this company? What does she want right now? What are the pressures on her? How much cash does she need to deploy? What are her KPIs? And so, we started to design buying experiences very much focused on an individual, and that's when we really started to grow.

It was a nine-year journey with lots of ups and downs. The scaling of a people business has its own unique challenges because our product is not something physical or digital, but rather the work done by a team. And so, we had to figure out how to be a large headcount company, even though we were still a small company. Those challenges came very quickly. We had a hundred full-time employees 6 to 8 months after starting. And with a lot of people comes a lot of a lot of people issues.

In the first year, I was very focused on revenue, and I thought that if you were making revenue in the business, everything would be taken care of. I hired all these people, but we had barely gotten paid at all by customers – some of whom had sixty-to-ninety-day payment terms. That's when I started understanding that cash flow was everything that our growing business was built on. And there's an inflection point when you really start to have a lot of cash flow. For example, you have to hire a human resource person, who can serve 40 people, but you need to hire them when you have five people. There is this kind of inefficiency built into the business until we hit an inflection point. The problem was that it took us way longer to hit an inflection point than I expected – I was just a 20-something year old and I had no exposure to managing cash flow during my time working in big firms. So, we kept burning through cash which was very stressful.

Early on I realized that if I'm not doing the selling, if I'm not talking to customers, this thing is not going to work. So, I picked up the phone and just started calling. Sometimes, I would email somebody in a city and say, hey, I'm coming through town. And only if they would confirm the meeting, then I book my flight. I started doing a lot of that. My day-to-day was really heavy on the customer side. I would say my side job was operations and actually running the business – but I had put together a really great team that was working day and night to deliver.

We took on some debt. I had a business partner in the business at the time. He eventually exited, but he put a little debt into the business. I funded our business through my personal savings and some family loans. We just propped it up. Cash flow was a three-year headache before we really started to make money.

But the good thing is, we survived that, and the gross margins in this in this space are 50-60%. We targeted an EBITDA of 20%. When I sold the company, we were doing 23% in EBITDA. We were a very profitable business, but if you don't hit that inflection point, you just burn out.

Even five years in, I was still very much customer focused. But that's when I realized that I'm not the CEO of this company right now. I am the head of sales, or I'm the chief human resource officer. I needed to be the CEO. I needed to actually put that hat on and do the real job of being CEO because we were at a size where I needed to do that. I really feel like I only promoted myself to that role after we were able to build a real sales engine.

Two or three years before our exit, I realized that I needed to start thinking about building an executive team to really take the business to the next level. Some hires didn't work out. I hired four or five senior-level sales directors until we realized that we needed to actually build a very strong sales process first. Now I realize there are multiple phases in hiring salespeople in a growing company, and at each phase you need a different type of profile – I had to learn that the hard way. Take what I'm doing and take what's in my head and put it into a process. I took a step back and really put the company at the forefront and made the company stand on its own. This was only possible with some key leadership hires who knew how to help me do this. Codifying what I was doing, especially when it came to customers but really all roles, became critical when it was time to sell the company because a lot of the potential buyers had to be convinced that without "Patrick" the business could still thrive. And by the time we sold we proved that the business really almost didn't need me at that point.

I landed on the fact that I really enjoyed certain phases of building the company. I didn't love it as much when I was a CEO of a thousand-person business. I felt like I kind of created my own corporate job. I have told many people I think running a really good business at level is actually quite boring, and it should be boring because when it's boring, it means things are working, we're disciplined, we're proactive and not firefighting all the time - and that's good.

The COO I eventually hired was much better at it than I was. She was so good at building systems that could scale out with the business' growth, very disciplined and organized, putting systems and processes in place. Same with the other executives I hired at that level in delivering services and finance. I recognized that, and I didn't really have any ego attached to being CEO of this company. For me, I was just very proud that the company was very successful and was working. And so, when the offer came along to buy the company outright, and for me to step down, it was like, "Yeah, I think that's the right decision for the company."

Also, as an entrepreneur, the creation of a new business and growth is the exciting part. It's creating something out of nothing and creating incredible career opportunities for people. My next venture takes a page out of what I've done in services and scaling people businesses, but this time I am fascinated by all the new AI tools out there that – when combined with people – can create better experiences than people alone can deliver. I enjoyed the process of M&A so much that now I'm looking at how do I grow my new business by acquiring other companies, and eventually helping many founders have exit opportunities like I had. I feel like I've been through so much, and learned through experiences and hard knocks, that my tool kit is well honed for building profitable tech-enabled services business.

Chapter 12

Carl Meier

Carl Meier started his career after college, working in nonprofits and then in banking. He decided banking wasn't for him, so he took a job at the daycare where two of his three kids were. However, his love of beer and his homebrewing hobby eventually led him to co-found Black Abbey Brewery and a taproom connected to the brewery, which is still in operation today.

After college, one of my college buddies said, "We should try to figure out how to make beer." We bought Charlie Papazian's book, *The New Complete Guide to Homebrewing*, and we were trying to figure it out. There was a little homebrew shop in my hometown. I bought malt extract, pellets, and a turkey fryer. I feel like people who have hobbies, many of them, have a sort of similar experience. Although I can buy this sort of lowest common denominator ingredient kit, the beer's not good. Well, how can we make it better?

My wife and I moved to Connecticut, and I continued to brew there. We were in an apartment, so it was kind of difficult. And then, from Connecticut, we moved on campus at Vanderbilt. We had a smaller apartment, and so it was even more complicated. And then, after Sally graduated from nursing school, we moved into a duplex. Now we've got a little more space. I bought more equipment. And next thing you know, I'm doing all-grain mash.

I joined a homebrew club at Bosco's[12] called the Music City Brewers. At the first meeting, I sat next to this cat, the treasurer, who was an accountant. His name is Ken Redman. Ken now runs Czann's Brewing. I sat next to this dude, Steve Scoville, who started Little Harpeth Brewing. At that meeting was Karen Lasseter, who went on to become the head brewer at Bosco's and then Corsair when they had a beer program. And Linus Hall, who started Yazoo. We were like the Music City mafia of beer at that time. It was ridiculous. Five of us went on into professional brewing!

But at that time, it was just fun. We were absolutely goofing off. We won a silver medal in the largest homebrew competition in the world in 2009 with

---

[12] Bosco's was a brew pub restaurant in Nashville that closed in 2014 after trying to weather the Great Recession.

a Belgian-style barrel-aged beer. We were going to Covenant Presbyterian. I met a fellow parishioner, Mike Edgeworth, who also was a home brewer. Mike said, "Why aren't you trying to sell this for money?" I said, "Well, John[13] and I had started a business plan. Then we tabled it. He got a new job. My wife and I were pregnant with number three. And man, it's a lot of money to start."

We both had regular jobs. We just didn't have the time or the money. Mike said, "Well, let's put some methodology to it. Let's start sitting down every Thursday night and working on a business plan." And so we did. I would brew beer. John would brew beer. We'd say, "What do we think about this? What do we think about that?" And then, we would work on the plan.

The Brewers Association had just come out with a book that was a manual of how to start your own brewery that we used to figure out if we could make this into a viable business entity and how much money we would need. We did that for the better part of two years. We had been doing that for a long time.

One night brewing, I got to thinking as we were brewing some Belgian-style beer that the Belgian beers were brewed by monks. Martin Luther was a monk. I'm on Wikipedia reading about Martin Luther. I'm fascinated by history and the quirkiness of history. After Luther was excommunicated, he married a nun named Catherine. Catherine exercised the brewery rights on this piece of property they were given as a wedding gift called the Black Cloister. It was where Luther had written the Ninety-five Theses. So, the monastery where he became a monk later became his homestead. She effectively financed his ministry by making beer in the monastery where Luther started as a monk. Right. Beer literally changes the world! I texted Mike and John in the middle of the night and said, "I've got it! We should call it the Black Cloister Brewing Company!"

The next morning, John texted back and said, "Drink three beers and try to say cloister." The kind of beer Catherine made in the Middle Ages is not what we like. What she would have been making would have been more akin to a Belgian or Abbey style of ale. So we put those two things together. Alright, now we've got a name. We've got a brand identity. We can start building a book of beers that fit under that European-influenced American craft beer umbrella. Now, the pieces are starting to fall into place. A friend of John's was an amateur graphic artist. He came up with the logo, and we

---

[13] John Owen, Carl's eventual business partner in Black Abbey Brewing.

sent it to the trademark office to get federal trademark protection. The last thing I wanted to do was go to a capital raise only to have the name and the brand all change.

We started our capital raise in 2011, and it took just shy of 12 months. In the beginning, I was going to run the pitch, John would run the numbers, and Mike brought us the people. Mike's a physician (a neurologist). He brought in a couple of people, and then John and I started asking around, and that was how we got the capital raise done.

Our leadership team has changed a lot over time. At first, we were meeting all the time. John and I were active, and we were in here all day, all night, every day. Mike has a professional career doing something else. And so, Mike would be in on the weekends and would do some stuff at night. And that was complicated because we would talk and make sort of freehand decisions about things and then have to bring Mike up to speed. We didn't necessarily have a determined schedule for when those things would happen. That's when we started doing what we call the Waffle House Summit, Friday mornings, two or three times a month. We would meet at Waffle House and talk about what was going on.

The way that our "Trinitarian setup" works is that I'm doing sales, John runs the inside of the building, and Mike is the quiet partner who sort of mediates disagreement to help us reach consensus. Mike oftentimes comes in as a fresh set of eyes. This is really helpful because both John and I can get lost in the trees. We don't see the forest. We live in silos. I'm in sales. John lives in production and logistics, where everything is black or white. Those views don't always line up. And, you know, our schedules are odd. John opens the brewhouse. He gets here early in the morning. A lot of my job happens in the afternoons and evenings. That's good for how our lives work. He doesn't like crowds. He doesn't like to talk in front of people. I like crowds. I love to talk in front of people. I'm very happy to sit down at a bar next to a complete stranger and strike up a conversation, thinking about how I'm going to get this guy to drink our beer and take it home with him.

***

Ten years ago, I think we really had this idea that we could be Sweetwater or Terrapin. We could be a regional player. Pretty quickly, we realized that the amount of work and the amount of money that that was going to take was really unreasonable. There's a brewery in Memphis, Wiseacre, that opened almost to the day we did. Wiseacre is now in 21 states. I know nothing about how their internal operations work. I don't know how their business is set up. But I can infer that they are significantly more well-capitalized than we are. Bart Watson, the chief economist for the Brewers Association, says that the way to make a small fortune in brewing is to start with a large fortune. Margins are tight, labor is difficult and expensive, and marketing doesn't ever stop. The other day, after my small group at church, I was off to a bar to hand out stickers and pint glasses for 2 hours. Why? Because I got to. Somebody has to.

Certainly, twelve years ago, I would have said, "You know, I just want to be big." And then you realize to get that big is going to require way more debt than any of us have. Ten years from now? Lord only knows. We've seen such radical change in the industry in the last ten years. I can only expect more radical change. When we opened, there were just shy of 2,000 breweries in the United States. Now, there are just shy of 10,000. Everybody's got a brewery within 15 miles of where they live. Like, you can go look at tanks anywhere. What's different is the story. What's different is the liquid. It used to be like were super unique. It was all about being in a brewery where you can smell it and see it. And now, everything's a gimmick. I was just offered a second taproom over on the west side. It doesn't look anything like what I would anticipate. It looks like a super cool lounge, and it's dark, and it's cool. Black Abby's gimmick was "church" in terms of stained-glass windows and the altar.

Change is a challenge. And how do you stay fresh, right? If I had the answer to that, I'd be in.

***

As a parent, I think about my kids and how they look at me when I'm home and when I'm not home. I think about how much weight I've gained since I started doing this and how much beer I drank.

My oldest is about to go to college in the fall. She'll go, and she'll get her degree. And if she comes to me one day and says, "Dad, I'm thinking about starting a business." What would I say? It's probably the same thing I would have said to "the Carl" of 2008. You need to really think about it because it's way more work than anybody would ever think. There's no way to be prepared for it. It's way more money than anybody would ever think. And it just becomes a constant need. And the risk, you know, the stuff that my name is on.

But, I'm very hesitant to say don't do it because I love what I do, and I love this industry, and I love beer. I specifically love the culture and personality of beer, the history of beer, and the art of beer. So, I think I would still want to try to somehow be involved in that. But I would tell myself back then that you might want to go work for a brewery before you just start one.

My story is the story of 8,000 other breweries stories. Mike, John, and I, we knew how to make good homebrew, and we thought we knew a little bit about branding and marketing, which turns out we really didn't know very much about that either. Beer is funny that way.

Chapter 13

Travis Contreras

Travis Contreras learned how to paint when he was a teenager in Columbus, Georgia, working for a woman who was a solo painter. When he turned eighteen, he applied to the military and the police academy. He decided to pursue a career in law enforcement, starting out as a cadet working in evidence.

I turned 21 while I was in the police academy. I was never going to leave. This was my career. I made really jam-up cases, and the detectives started looking at me in my third year, and they said, "Hey, we're looking at you for Special Operations."

I spent three years as a special operations, high crime officer. We had two units. There was the high crime unit. It was a uniformed unit where our daily goal was to go out in the city. We would go to the worst parts of town and find anyone breaking the law. Normally, we got people on dope, guns, and stuff like that. We would work some vice crimes, prostitution, but we would just go out and enforce the law in high crime areas very, very rigorously. We were arresting multiple people a day for very heinous crimes. Toward the end, your body starts hurting because you're getting in multiple foot pursuits a day, multiple altercations a day, and adrenaline dumps 24/7.

My command came to me and said, "We've seen your work. We've definitely seen your reports. We're looking at you to be a special agent."

So, I did plainclothes undercover for an additional three years, and that was great. It was like my dream as a kid that I wanted to be one of those guys. And undercover was great, man. I truly loved it, but I felt like that was my peak. Toward the end of undercover, I just got burned out. You're hanging out with drug dealers and prostitutes. I went to my commander and asked, "Where do you think I should go next?"

And she said, "Travis, I have never recommended a male for this position, but I think you should work in sex crimes." I've got three kids. I've never thought about doing this position.

I transferred to sex crimes. And it was one of the most rewarding things I ever did with my life, helping a child in a position they cannot get out of.

ENTREPRENEURIAL VOICES

Helping an adult in a position that they cannot get out of. Hearing the stories of sexual abuse, stories of children that had been abused since they were 12. And now they're 18 or 19. And it's all true. We were interviewing the suspects and just sitting there with them, knowing we had them. I would just put my hand on their back, saying, "Hey, let's pray together."

The intense investigations to get a true criminal, a true predator, off the street was so rewarding to me. Then a realization came to me. I'm sitting at my desk, working on this case for days and days. Because in those cases, when you have evidence, you can't go home. There's no going home because a lot of that evidence is serological. And if you don't get it, if you don't collect it, it's gone. When I was tired, I would go home and decompress from all the stuff I had just witnessed, and watched, and heard. And then we got a call out, and it was another brutal one.

I got back to my desk and sat down. I had gotten my check, and it was $2,200, just like it was every other month. And then it just hit me so quickly. I started thinking about all my days on patrol, where I worked my tail off and worked circles around all the other guys making the same check. I got to go to Special Ops, but they're making the same money. You're doing undercovers. You're not going home. And I sat there at my desk, and I was like, "Man, I am working circles around so many other officers in this department, making the exact same money. What am I doing? What am I doing?"

So, I went to my sergeant and said, "I think I'm starting a painting company."

And he said, "Travis, I don't know. I don't know if it's a good idea. You've got 13 years, and you're being groomed to go places here. You're highly sought after. I don't know if that's a good choice. What about retirement? You're the age now that maybe this isn't the time to jump off a cliff. So, what's your business plan?"

I said, "Well, I'm going to go see if I can buy a truck. If I can buy a truck, I'm going to quit and start a business."

So, I left work that day. I went to Ford, and I bought a truck for $15,000. It just felt right. It felt so right. I bought the truck, and that was my answer. I get chills now thinking about it. I risked everything. I've got three kids! But it worked out so well. Little did I know what came with business ownership at the time. I do not have a single entrepreneur in my family.

I've never seen the personal struggles of owning a business, but I started my business, I became a painter. Paint Ops was born!

I spent two weeks going to estimates that I generated from my launch. My launch was creating a Facebook post saying, "Hey, guys. You all know and love me. I'm a painter. Please recommend my company. I'm quitting the police department." I got four or five leads from that.

I made a spreadsheet that had a Paint Ops logo on it. When I went to a bid, I'd write notes and look at them with extreme confidence that I could take care of this for them. There was a lot of falling forward, but I never stopped. Finally, I landed a bid. I remember installing a printer in my truck and customers were always so shocked that they had a printed estimate detailed with their home's needs.

I wanted to be as professional as possible because all my local competition was just very poor, smelling like alcohol and showing up in disheveled clothes. I genuinely wanted to do a good job, and I genuinely wanted my customers to feel that they just had someone that they could eat dinner in their homes. That's what I have preached to all my guys. Before hiring someone, I say, "Hey, read my reviews. Because if that don't sit you down and let you know I'm not playing with how well I want to take care of my customers, then you don't need to work here."

When I get a review, they write paragraphs and paragraphs and paragraphs about us in their home. And it is just, it's a beautiful thing to see. The guys working with me feel like they come to work with family every day. And their happiness, it goes with our homeowners. I'll say, "Hey, guys, stop what you're doing. Our homeowner just got home with groceries. We're bringing in their groceries."

We have weekly huddle sessions, and we just talk about life experiences. A lot of emotional-based stuff like, "Hey, how did it make you feel when that homeowner came home and gave you dinner because you helped them with the groceries?" And they're like, "Dude, honestly, simply picking up a bag changed my life. How many more people just need a small gesture of kindness?" And I'm showing them what's possible through just being a great human being, just truly pouring yourself out to others without an ask back. We're not asking them for something. We're carrying groceries. We're helping. We had one client lose a dog. We spent three hours going through the woods to find this dog. We truly just want to be there for our clients.

Every one of my guys has contacted me to work for me. I've not put up a single job ad. Each of them said, "Hey, man, I saw your videos. I've heard great things about Paint Ops. I would love to work under you." I've only done three interviews. Hired all of them and they are still with me. My main guy, Christian, he's been with me since the beginning.

What I want is massive success in my company to be able to massively help my community. I bought a bunch of Chick-Fil-A cards recently, about $500 worth. I'll go to Starbucks, and if I see a mom smiling at her kids, I get the Chick-Fil-A card and say, "You are an incredible mother. And the way your daughter looks at you, that lunch is on me." And that's peanuts. And I'm able to do that because of what I've created.

I show up to an estimate with a list of twelve charities, and I say, "If you do decide to go with me, please pick from one of these before I leave. And a portion of my personal profit is going to go to one of these."

My ultimate goal is to have ten painters and be a $1.2 million company. I can take care of my people and take care of my children with that. If God puts in my path, "Hey, Travis, you know what? I actually want you to juggle $10 million because I think you can do more with $10 million than with $1 million," I'm here for it.

I used to bring a gun to work, and now I bring a paintbrush to work and can provide more for my family by bringing a paintbrush to work. It makes no sense at all. But I can do so much more for my family right now with a paintbrush than I could as a police officer. And it's crazy because all these people I helped, especially the sex crime stuff. I know I was doing something good, but I also wanted to provide more for my family. It was truly one of the hardest decisions I have ever made.

I got a call one day to bid on Manchester High School. At the time, I only had two guys, and one of the guys had never painted before. Ever! Mind you, we haven't done a commercial job like this. When I got to the high school, paint was coming off in sheets. And I'm thinking, "Holy crap, how do you price sandblasting an entire school? Like, how do you do that?"

My buddy Christian said, "Dude, I never saw you sweat."

And I said, "Dude, you can't let him see you sweat. We're all in this bid."

He said, "How do you price something like this?"

I said, "We're about to figure it out, Christian. We're going to figure it out right now."

So, we go through the bid. We have two options. I can bid this to sandblast the entire school and get all this paint off. The cost for that is going to be abhorrent, and the school is going to be filled with dust. Or we can peel back, prime, and repaint with a really high-structured epoxy. We chose to bid that one. I wrote a bid for $44,500. My true costs came in right at $40,000.

I said, "Can you show me the bids from the other painter?" She shows me, and it's at $44,000 even. She said that they didn't test anything, they didn't say they were scraping, and they didn't say they would prime. They just said $44,000 and walked out. Knowing so early on that I am competing with other companies and coming in with similar and market numbers was such a great feeling, it was proof to myself that I was honing the craft of entrepreneurship.

She says, "Look, I want you." So, she filmed the rest of the bid and presented it to the school board. And I got a $44,500 bid.

Me, Christian, and Zachariah walked into the school. And I looked at them and said, "You guys, I promise you, take as many breaks as you want. I will not stop. I will not stop from the time we get here until the time we leave. And I want you guys to watch me work. Don't feel discouraged. If you get tired, and you're going to get tired, go take a break. But I want you to see how big this job is for Paint Ops and how much it means to me."

We got that school done, the three of us, in 15 days.

I got in my truck and said, "Oh, my God, it is possible. If you put yourself in the right place at the right time with the right people, it is possible." Like, I literally have chills right now thinking about it.

I think there are different kinds of wins. And, you know, some of the early ones for a lot of us are the ones that mean the most. They're the ones that give us that confidence. And I can tell you now, it was worth it. It means much more working tirelessly as the proprietor of Paint Ops than waiting on that government check. Now, when I give the output, I get the return.

I didn't have a business plan, no savings, and I didn't even have a loan. I got that truck and just drove to bids. That was it.

Chapter 14

Robert Riggs

Robert began his career working in the U.S. Congress as an aide and then as a congressional investigator. He then moved into journalism, spending the next thirty years as a bureau chief and investigative reporter. Then, in 2008, the recession gutted television news, and he found himself out of work, about to become one of many accidental entrepreneurs who emerged from that economic downturn. Robert was always fascinated by technology. He saw an opportunity to turn his interests into a business.

So, my wife compares life as the days of TV money and the days now post TV money. Because in those days, the networks are very flush with money. And if you had risen up the chain, you were handsomely paid. And in a split second, it went away, was gone. I got a severance, but I had two kids in college and a huge mortgage.

The saving grace for me was that I've always been a techie at heart. At CBS, I had started a blog about terrorism. I started this in 2004 after I came back from the war. My producer and I decided we were going to focus on terrorism and start a blog about it. CBS hated it. But we were killing it. I had in excess of 20,000 people around the world following the intelligence agencies.

I actually found out that none of the CBS websites were getting indexed by Google. And I went to Google and got them to index the site. These were the days when you could game search engine optimization with keywords. It was all an experiment. I had lots of success doing that.

And so here I am, out of work. What am I going to do? Well, I hung out a shingle as an Internet media and marketing expert.

I took my severance package, and I went out and traveled around the country, going to Internet marketing and SEO conferences and trying to learn more about it. I actually went out to California, and I met Vint Cerf, who was one of the three creators of the Internet.

The other thing I didn't know anything about was running a business. In my previous career, I'd worked in Congress and big media. Everything's taken care of there. I knew I needed to learn. And I went to the University of Texas at Dallas. They had an entrepreneurship certification program.

I continued doing consulting. I made mediation videos for personal injury law firms where you tell the story of the victim, and they use it for settlement purposes to keep cases out of court. I was also doing freelance writing for executives and top financial agents.

I've always been a storyteller and love telling stories. That's what I loved in journalism. And when podcasting was coming of age, I watched it and studied it. People kept saying to me, you really ought to do a podcast about your stories.

My wife had said, "You need to do true crime. The stories you did reporting in crime were incredible." The audience spoke, and they loved it. The numbers were phenomenal. That's the interesting thing about the Internet. You can hear from the audience. On the Internet, my podcast, I get analytics on how long they listen to that. Where they quit. So, I dug my reporter's notebooks out of the attic and started a podcast. Retired FBI agents and retired officers were free to talk now.

I wrote a business plan. Who is the audience? What are they interested in? Where do I find them? How am I going to make money out of this? And I had a whole list of the revenue options for making money. Ads in the podcast. Affiliate marketing. I looked at all aspects of how to make money. At the bottom of the list was television. Spin it off into TV shows. It seemed like a long shot. But I produced a 17-part series about a notorious serial killer that most people have never heard of, named Kenneth McDuff. I played a big role, an investigative role, in exposing that he got out of prison under a cloud of corruption. I assembled the key members of the investigation and got all the interviews in the can.

And then the pandemic hit. In one week, I lost every client I had because everyone closed up. The personal injury lawyers I was working with closed the courthouses and closed up some of the judgments. They didn't think they were going to get paid. They were hanging on for dear life. And, as the freelancer, you're the first thing to go. So suddenly, I had plenty of time to work on the project.

I had everything in the can. I had everything done and started working on it. I got PPP[14] money, and that really helped pay the rent.

---

[14] PPP was the Paycheck Protection Program, which provided small businesses with resources to maintain their payroll, hire back employees, and cover

I started posting the episodes. I knew I had to get it into Apple, Spotify, Podcaster, and everywhere else. I put up on LinkedIn that this was coming out. I started getting contacted by people I didn't know personally, but they knew of me from my career in journalism, and they were involved with podcasting. By the sixth episode, the president of Big Media contacted me. He started asking very detailed questions, and I knew, "Oh, he's listening."

We did a co-production agreement. With that papered and that agreement done, I helped them prepare more information, the pitch, and everything about it. One of the things that happened in this period that was fortunate for me is that there was a moment during the pandemic when streaming and the TV world thought, "Oh, my God, we're all going to go under."

Then, the first quarterly results came in for Netflix, and they had a huge increase in revenue because everybody was home. This set off an alarm among many other companies that thought, "Oh, my God, we got to get in this game, or they're going to own all the content. They're going to have all the viewers."

Suddenly, demand just blew wide open for good content. I was a benefactor of luck and circumstance there. Being at the right place. I'm a firm believer that you don't get to the right place unless you're really working at it. There is luck involved, but it doesn't happen unless you're working hard at it.

So, it got picked by Fox Nation streaming. It's a streaming channel at Fox, and it was a kind of a new endeavor for them. We were the first production done outside the company, and the stars really all aligned. The crew that came together to work with me felt like I was back with my best group from when I was in television news. We all spoke the same language. There were no big egos in the room. We all had complementary talents.

The show premiered in March of last year. It was a hit, and within two months, it won a Telly Award, and it's up for some more awards now. Five episodes, about 45 minutes each. It's a $1,750,000 production for five episodes that didn't go into Robert's pocket.

We wanted not to look like any crime show you'd ever seen. We had a different approach, and it was shot like a movie. The show opens with

---

applicable overhead during COVID.

deputies on horseback like a posse, an old-style oil pump jack, and an old-style windmill turning. And because we wanted to tap what we saw coming with the popularity of Yellowstone. And it worked.

We have pivoted to produce audiobooks and are currently working on our first anthology, "Tales of Murder, Mayhem, and Mystery from Inside the Crime Scene Tape" by True Crime Reporter®.

I, along with my talented producer Seiler Burr have developed an "immersive audio experience" that creates a compelling experience for the listener. Books are written for the eye, and I don't think they translate to the spoken word media. In television and radio, you write for the ear.

My wife and I studied classic crime shows from the golden age of radio and the detective stories of Agatha Christie and Raymond Chandler, among others, to infuse creativity into our audio stories.

The podcast enables us to experiment and learn what connects with the audience. It also serves as an authoritative source of information so people understand that they can trust me for accuracy, fairness, and sensitivity.

Many independent creators like me are working on ways to directly connect with their audience. Building a business on Meta, TikTok, YouTube, and other channels is "sharecropping." Growing up in East Texas, I saw what happened to poor black and white farmers who tried to grow crops on another landowner's property. Thus, we use the podcast to help build an email list and feature our own products.

It has never been harder to build an audience online. The number of podcasts regularly producing episodes is on a rapid decline. Even Prince Harry and Meghan failed.

In this atmosphere, I adopted a "what's old is new approach." I turn my podcast episodes into true crime newspaper stories and give them to publishers needing content. In return, they allow me to promote my podcast with links and a QR code to help grow my audience.

I now use artificial intelligence tools as my creative research and writing assistant. If you know how to harness the applications, you can use your time more efficiently. In the wake of AI, I believe that proving "you are who you say you are" online and not a synthetic creature is a new challenge.

In this connection, the two principal producers of "Freed To Kill," my television documentary about serial killer Kenneth McDuff, are guiding the production of a true crime stage show conducted in front of a live audience.

It's titled "Manhunt: Take Down of a Serial Killer," featuring true crime stories and lessons in personal safety.

My mission is twofold. First, tell stories that convey the professionalism, dedication, and humanity of the men and women in the criminal justice system. And second, educate the public with skills to avoid and survive criminal acts. I am launching an Apple Subscription channel with a feature called Behind the Badge: Outwitting Threats with Streetwise Survival Skills. We decode the subtle signs of crime, sharpen our street smarts, and empower ourselves with the knowledge that could one day save a life.

Suppose you could talk to Robert in 2008 when everything fell apart. Knowing what you know now, what advice would you give yourself as you face this new stage in your career?

Do some things earlier. Don't procrastinate on them. Jump in and do it. Realize that you're going to probably have to pivot. Don't study it to death. I'll give you an example. There was a gentleman, Gary Leland, one of the pioneers in podcasting. He made a ton of money in podcasting. He started a podcast about girls fastpitch softball. It exploded. Who was the audience? The dads who wanted their daughters to be successful.

He started using the podcast as a vehicle to sell manuals that he put out on Amazon. Everything from how to play first base, how to play shortstop, how to bat. He also started selling his own branded equipment.

Gary kept saying to me, "Robert, with all your stories. Get off your butt. Get this podcast going."

I wish I had started the podcast three years earlier. I could have.

Chapter 15

Todd Tietgens

Todd Tietgens and I talked about his lifelong experience in a family business in the kitchen of his home in rural Lewisburg, Tennessee. Todd got started in the family grocery store business when he was a teenager. His dad had had a successful career with SuperValu. However, he had had enough of "the corporate life." The family joked that their dad was in the "corporate army" because they moved a lot. His dad decided to shift gears and buy a grocery store in a small town called Rainsville in North Alabama. Todd was sixteen. He and his fourteen-year-old brother immediately went to work in the store. They worked forty hours a week with their dad to help build the family business.

I worked so much in high school and through college that I thought, you know, the only thing I don't want when I get out of school is to work in a grocery store! I thought with my connections that I had a good chance to get a job with Kraft Foods. But in 1982-83, Kraft was going through a thing where you had to have minority status to even apply for a position. When that didn't work out, I got some other job offers. One was in Chicago, and one was in Texas. They would have been good jobs, but they were "suit and tie every day" kind of jobs, and I didn't want to really live in a big city. It was a tough economy and wasn't like it is today. You had to have an "in" to get a good job.

My dad had an opportunity to open another store. So, on my last day of class in college, I moved to Rockwood, Tennessee. I had never been there, never seen it, didn't know a soul. So, he dropped me off, and I had to go get my own apartment. I went to work two days later. Two days after my last class, I was working in his new store.

I was assistant manager and trying to learn because I'd done the assistant manager stuff in his first store, but I always had somebody that knew what to do. I was just kind of thrown into it.

My dad had gotten an opportunity to sell his store in Rainsville. He bought a different store in Columbia, Tennessee. In 1983, a headhunter found him and offered him a job in Nashville, back in the wholesale business that he knew. He was able to buy some ownership in it. He still owned the store in Columbia and the store in Rockwood. I was trying to learn my lessons there that I needed to progress.

In 1984, we bought a third store in Livingston, Tennessee. I was the manager there. And in 1985, we bought a store in McMinnville, Tennessee. After that, I went into the supervisor role. I was managing the Livingston store while overseeing the other three stores. That was probably over my head, but it worked out.

My one brother graduated in 1986, I believe, and he went into financial planning. He did that for ten years.

My youngest brother got out of college in 1988. We were building a new store in Mount Pleasant, Tennessee, when he was getting out. He went to work for us in our McMinnville store as assistant store manager. And then, when the Mount Pleasant store opened, he ran that store.

After that, we bought store number six in Lawrenceburg, Tennessee. And then, we built a store in Summertown, Tennessee. So, we were running seven stores at one time.

We can't compete with the programs of the big employers. We offer our store managers a percentage of the profits. Everybody is not the key employee, but you've got to look at your key employees and find out what their needs are. Most people want to be recognized, and they want to have a stake in it. My dad started giving managers a bonus percentage. So, when they're spending your money, they're spending their own money. And when they're making you money, they're making their money based on a decent salary with a percentage of profits. They don't have to actually own. But it's like ownership, and they feel it's like ownership without the investment. And, you know, that's worked for us.

We offer flexible schedules. They're like family to us. The main group of employees really feel like that's their store, too. And that's what we want. It's not just my brothers and my parent's family; it's the whole family. So, everybody there is family to me. If they need something, and we can help them, we have helped. We can make their life a little easier. My parents were real big about that. My mother would go in the first time we bought a store and just make people feel at ease.

My brother, who did financial planning, decided he was interested in coming into the family business. I said, "Well, you have to go see Dad about it, but we'd be happy to have you if you want to come."

My youngest brother and I weren't making any money at the time because we were just employees, but we were starting to at least be able to get by. My other brother had been out for so long that he had a ways to go to learn the business. And he dug in and learned it in Lawrenceburg.

When did you and your brothers get ownership in the business?

In the previous year or two, I'd gone to see my dad and said I'd like to buy into the business. And he said, "Well, you know, you don't have any money."

I said, "It's because I'm working for you!"

We sat down with Dad and talked to him about it. He was a fair guy and worked it out for us so we could buy into the business with sweat equity and with reinvesting the money that we made in bonuses.

My dad grew up in a tough era, and we weren't about borrowing money. We did things as we could pay for them. And right or wrong, it worked for us. In hindsight, maybe we should have borrowed money. But, you know, I can't argue. I mean, it's been way better than we ever thought it would be.

In 2010, my mom was getting sick. She had congestive heart disease. Dad gave us an opportunity to buy the buildings that we didn't have already. He sold them at a very reasonable price. He financed it with no bank, with nobody else involved. We got those paid off in 2019. Dad still had some investment in the grocery company, but he wasn't really involved in the day-to-day. My mom passed away in 2010, and he took that hard. We were all doing okay. He'd still call, but it wasn't like it used to be. He had trust in us then, and we were making it work. He was taking care of his kids, and we were taking care of him. So, it was kind of a good thing.

There's a sense of accomplishment, and we've gotten way farther along than I ever dreamed of when I was a kid. It's the amazing trips through the business over the years (back when wholesalers still did that kind of thing). We would never have gotten to do any of that stuff: China, Hong Kong, and a lot of places in Europe. We would have never been exposed to that kind of thing. We worked hard, including my kids, since they were twelve. They worked with me on Christmas Day. It was a family thing. We were open on Christmas Day, and that's probably our biggest day of the year. The employees get extra pay, but they don't have to work. I've worked 34 Christmas days. It wasn't always my wife's happy day, but it was really my favorite day at work because everybody was in a good mood. We'd hear,

"You saved my Christmas!" Obviously, Christmas wasn't really going to be destroyed if they didn't get those dinner rolls or whatever they needed. If everybody could keep that attitude... The next day was back to normal. But on that day, I never saw an unhappy person. It was kind of nice.

What does the future hold for your family grocery business?

Everybody thought the videotape movie rentals were going to be there forever. And even newspapers. Newspapers used to be where we drove sales. And that's why we stayed in the rural markets because we couldn't afford the newspaper ads in the bigger cities. And when COVID hit, we couldn't run a newspaper. We transitioned to digital ads and away from newspapers because, during COVID, we didn't know what we were going to get. So, we couldn't have an ad. I remember a conversation I had with my daughter. When Pat Summitt [famed University of Tennessee women's basketball coach] died, I said, "Sarah, pick up a couple newspapers on Pat Summitt. We'll save them."

About two hours later, she called and said, "Where do you get a newspaper?"

All of this home delivery is coming on. We have not gotten into home delivery yet. That's not saying that we won't do it, but we're in rural markets. Some of our customers might be ten miles out. We don't have a concentrated core of customers.

That's the scary part. What can it do? How long can it last? What if something else changes? It was a big risk for me to put everything my family has into this business, and then all of a sudden, it just goes the way of the dinosaur. So, you know, we don't know. We're just going to run it as long as we can and then see what happens.

Chapter 16

Adam Bedwell

I first met Adam and his wife, Tyler (whose story is in another chapter), at my favorite local taproom. A random conversation at the corner of the bar left me excited to learn more about each of their entrepreneurial journeys.

I had first started college at Freed-Hardeman University. I transferred to Harding University and majored in exercise science. Then, I went to Tennessee State University to get a doctorate in physical therapy. After graduating, I had failed the final test for the PT boards, which you need to get your license, twice. I had a job offer here in Cool Springs, Franklin, Tennessee, with Elite Physical Therapy. They waited on me after the first time I took the test, but after the second one, they hired somebody else. I was devastated. I hadn't passed the board yet after all this schooling. And I had thought that I was going to work for Elite forever.

I was trying to figure out what I was going to do with my life. So, this is when my story really starts. I was getting ready to take the boards a third time in October of 2012. I got a phone call from this girl I went to college with at Freed-Hardeman, named Becca. I knew she had married this guy named Brian Coggins. He had started this family-owned business, Prestige Physical Therapy, down in the south end of Tennessee in Waynesboro, Tennessee. Brian had been working at Vanderbilt but wanted to do his own thing. He went back home and started his company. There were no therapists down here.

On October 23rd, 2012, I took the boards for a third time. And then, on November 1st, I received my pass and got my license number. I drove down to join Brian in Waynesboro, Tennessee. We had one outpatient clinic and a contract with a non-skilled nursing home in Waynesboro. We also were doing some physical therapy home health for those who cannot get to an outpatient clinic. For example, your mother or your grandmother comes home after a knee replacement or hip replacement. They're homebound after a nursing home stay. Our therapist meets them in their home and does their therapy. When they get done, they discharge them from home health. After that, it is their choice to where they go. But, there are not many outpatient locations in our markets. Because they know you, they follow you to your clinic. So, we make income from their home care and then from outpatient.

Brian had started the company, but he needed that second PT to become the workhorse to get it growing. I'm not the numbers guy. I'm not the visionary. But I'll say this, I'm the one who kind of sped up our growth process. We started getting traction in the outpatient clinic, nursing home, and home care. We knew we had some type of unique business model. So, we tried it in another county. It started working.

Prestige now services over ten counties in Tennessee, from Maury County all the way to Hardeman County, which is almost to Memphis. There's not been any true magic to our growth. But I can say this: for these past ten years, any contract, any patient, any nursing home administrator, any person we've sat down with, we've just been upfront and honest. There's no "I'm going to promise you this. And your patients are going to get this much better." We just show up, and every time we say we would do something, we do it.

We started having to commute to West Tennessee, which is a two-hour one-way drive. I would see eight or nine patients and then drive two hours back home to Columbia in Middle Tennessee. I did that for about eight months. We got introduced to a therapist by the name of Jesse Gatlin. He was working in a hospital therapy job in Jackson, in West Tennessee. We presented Jesse with the kind of opportunity that Brian offered to me. Brian said, "I've got a vision. I've got a plan in all these counties. There's nobody out here. I need someone to partner with me to do this." So, Jesse is now a partner with us. He's not in the clinics but does all of the home care and manages that part of the business.

A big part of my job is about the relationships that we've created. If you look at the map, you'll see there just aren't a lot of physical therapy companies in our areas. A lot of it is that the big companies can't find therapists. Most of our therapists were once patients when they were high school students. We hired them as technicians. Then, they got encouraged to go to school. They came back home, and we hired them.

***

It was probably one of the worst phone calls. It was raining. I was driving out to Linden, Tennessee, to our clinic. Brian called me. We had brought on a guy to help us grow the business and to be that non-therapist to go around to have meetings. Brian said, "I think I'm on to something. I'm not accusing him, but I feel pretty confident that he is embezzling." Brian is very conservative, and he doesn't overdramatize. The person we hired had full access to our accounts -- everything. What's funny is that we met him through our West Tennessee therapist, Jesse. He was friends with Jesse at the time. Even so, things weren't looking right.

Brian ended up going straight to him. He had looked at the finances and accounts, and talked with our CPA. He completely confessed when Brian confronted him. He said, "I figured you and Adam were fine." He used our accounts as, and I had never heard this word, but a slush fund. Tens of thousands. He said, "I was going to repay the money." Brian said, "No, you won't. You never will."

I had a lot of reservations when Brian brought him in. But at the same time, and like I've explained to my wife when you're down in these rural areas, you really can't be picky, you can't be choosy, you need people to work. When we brought him on, he was fine. Anybody can change through the years and get greedy. But I always had my reservations. Jesse, Brian, and I all decided to fire him. We said, "You have a lot more to deal with in your own personal life. We will all want our money back." So, 2020 started with firing him. Oh, and by the way, his wife was working for us. We fired her, too. He threw away all of the opportunities he had with Brian and me all because he wanted a slush fund.

Now, the $50,000 he embezzled was detrimental to a small company. Yeah, Detrimental! But we got on fire after that. He's gone! Here we go! In February and March of 2020, we opened two outpatient clinics, number seven and eight, in Decatur County and in Columbia, my hometown.

So, we open clinics seven and eight, and then COVID hits. Everything in our company, basically the whole outpatient world, goes to telehealth and one-on-one. I mean, you couldn't do much of anything to make a dollar. We did the PPP[15] loan and were able to keep all of our therapists working. What got us through 2020 was our home health care. If you look back at our home health numbers, they actually increased during COVID. We still took a major hit on the clinic side, in nursing homes, and in the school systems. We lost all that.

I remember a conversation I had with Brian back in 2012. He said, "We

---

[15] Paycheck Protection Program (PPP) was a funding program during COVID to help small businesses and their employees when the government forced businesses to close due to the pandemic.

need to diversify ourselves." So, for the past ten years, that's what we've done. Who ever thought a pandemic would hit in 2020? And Brian said, "I know this year's going to be rough, but we would have been shut down if it weren't for the diversity that we established."

Then, in 2022, we lost seven people due to job, career, and family changes. We spent all of 2022 as a rebuilding year. You lose them, and guess how long it takes just to find another one. It was a constant turnover last year. All we did was just cover week to week, month to month. We still ended the year really well. Going into 2023, we hired a new PT and replaced all the people who left.

When I look back on my first few years, I see that I deal with stress and problems within the company differently today than when I was younger. I would take it personally when someone turned in their notice. Now, I think after the embezzlement, COVID, and now 2022, I've managed stress and difficulties very differently. The Adam I was just a few years ago is an extremely different person in terms of how I handle conflict today. I've come to learn that, at the end of the day, as good as anyone can be, they're going to do what's best for their family.

We have been approached by larger physical therapy companies. We've had a few meetings. We're not opposed to selling, partnering, whatever that may look like. It just doesn't seem with what we've been through, whether it was the embezzlement, COVID, or seven employees leaving like that, our gut feeling is that now's not the time.

In the next five years, we've got a group within the company that, if they want, can step up and become like an embedded partnership within the company. Brian and I want to give the opportunity to all of the people in this company and offer them a structure and a way to invest. What that does is it gives us the confidence in knowing these kids aren't leaving us.

I feel better about Prestige than I have in a while.

SECTION 3

SERENDIPITY

"There'll always be serendipity involved in discovery."
Jeff Bezos

Chapter 17

Ryan Pruitt

Ryan's early career was in music. He is a drummer, who traveled extensively throughout Europe playing in venues and music festivals. Like many musicians, he worked side jobs to get by. Many of his side jobs involved coffee shops, which offered benefits and flexibility. In 2006, Ryan started working at a coffee shop called Frothy Monkey, located in Nashville, TN. In 2008, when Ryan and his wife were expecting their first child, he decided it was time to move his restaurant work to full-time and his music to part-time. A few years later he approached the owner of Frothy Monkey about buying the restaurant. She was opening a new restaurant and was ready to put her efforts into that new venture. They came to terms and Frothy Monkey was now Ryan's to develop and grow. Today, Frothy Monkey has eight locations, a bakery, and a roasting company.

I didn't really view myself as an entrepreneur until fairly recently. The business that I own is one that I acquired after working there. I tell people all the time that I've not had that "come up with an idea, launch it, and on day one, see if anybody shows up to give you money" experience. But with each business (we've also launched a roasting company and a bakery), I'm now wrapping my head around, "Oh, that's the entrepreneurial spirit of what I've been doing."

We bought the business to expand it. The decisions we were making were "test driving" what we knew it would need to start expanding, or to solidify the brand experience. When I was working there, it was a typical early nineties coffee house: no cooking equipment, no hood, only microwaves, conveyor toasters, yogurt parfaits, oatmeal, muffins, coffee, a bunch of plants, minimal tables. That was the model. And now we are what we refer to as the "all-day cafe." It is breakfast, lunch, and dinner: coffee, tea, beer, wine, and cocktails. Open three meals a day, seven days a week. We are big believers that everyone's "coffee shop experience" doesn't just involve coffee and a muffin between 7:00 and 9:00 a.m. There is a "coffee shop experience" for a nurse that gets off a third shift; she wants a glass of wine at nine in the morning before going to bed. The freelance photographer who's doing that as a side hustle while working a day job; they need a coffee shop at 7:00 p.m. But they also need a good, nourishing, delicious dinner entree that's not 80 bucks and an environment where you can have a laptop out with a coffee or beer, whatever makes you better at photo editing. We cover all those grounds, and that's the way people use our buildings.

The second location was supposed to be downtown Nashville, in a building that I loved. We had a lease ready to sign, and then received a call from the building owner and he says, "You know, I have some bad news, or at least bad for you. I've got a dress boutique from New York City that's got a check in hand that wants the building and it's worth three times what you're willing to pay for it." No question mark there. Just a statement.

I woke up the next morning and said, "I remember the sign hanging at this house in downtown Franklin. I took a picture." I scrolled through my photos, and I found the for-lease sign. I made a phone call that morning. I met with them the next day and started the process for our downtown Franklin location. It is in the old minister's home of the Presbyterian Church in downtown Franklin. And it took 13 months to get that one open. There are a slew of reasons for this. I didn't know what I was doing. Our landlord was a church; they didn't know what they were doing regarding leasing property. Working in downtown Franklin became pretty difficult. Building codes in Nashville were hard, Brentwood was harder, and Franklin took the cake. Franklin is my hometown where I grew up, and the same for two of the partners at Frothy. It was a great part of our story to take the second location of Frothy, the first location our team built, to the town where we grew up. And it's been a great location.

Location three was in Nashville in a building that's around the corner from the lease that we lost through that same broker that was involved in the first one.

What was your typical day in the early days from the first location, maybe through that third location?

My typical day then consisted of three outfits. Literally, I would leave the house with a wardrobe bag. I would leave dressed for construction. I would go check on the downtown location that was under construction. And by check on it, I mean, I would be on my hands and knees running the tape measure and making sure everything's going to fit the way it's supposed to. I'm still very hands on like that during construction. I believe that's the way to do it if you want to have the finished product you want. So, I'm still running tape measures as we're building location number eight right now.

And then I would change clothes, pop over to Frothy on 12 South to get something to eat and check on the team there. We're a relationship driven company, so I'd see our customers and people I've known for years.

And then, I'd head out to the car, tuck in the shirt, throw the tie on, and go into the bank.

I always had three outfits in the car. Construction, bank meetings, and then my everyday wear. That's what a normal day looked like.

How did you approach growth from that point?

We have a team of people that keep growth at the forefront of our plans. We wanted to integrate our Coffee Roasting and BAKERY companies into the model. We wanted to continue to grow regionally as well as in our home city. But we wanted to do all of this in a sustainable way that holds onto the magic of that first location. That's when we decided to take the M&M approach to growth -- the money and managers -- the fact that you have to have both in order to take a stair step of growth. And that's how we make growth decisions.

Chattanooga was our first location out of Nashville. It also was the first time we opened two locations in one calendar year. They were six months apart: our Chattanooga store and our Nations store. We submitted the architectural plans to the city of Nashville for the Nations store on opening day in Chattanooga, and then it opened six months later.

That was our "oh shit" moment.

The company went from 70 employees to about 150 over the course of six months. We didn't have a great handbook in place. We didn't have a training program in place. We didn't have enough hands in place. Our financial systems were getting crushed. Going from 3 units to 5 units really stressed our bookkeeping. That was big, big growth for us, for sure!

We spent 2018 and 2019 learning how to operate what we have created for ourselves, beefing up our admin team, working on our processes, learning the beauty of systems, such as ops systems, and checklists. These are all bad words for entrepreneurs. You sit in meetings, and you start hearing, "This is going to make us too corporate." People work here because they don't want to work in corporate. And so we began that beautiful tension of having enough systems to set yourself up for success and some scale, but in a way that supports the creative and emotional leaders that we have in our company. We've spent so many hours learning how to balance it, and hiring for it, talking about it. Realizing that you can scale a company without losing its soul. Right. We didn't go out and hire someone who knew how to run twelve locations. We took the people who know how to "Frothy" really well, and then we've all learned how to set the business up to do its next steps, it's M&Ms, so that we can get back to growing in 2020.

We had a building under construction in East Nashville. It was an acquisition of an existing cafe in East Nashville, which is where I lived for 13 years. I was really passionate and protective of that neighborhood but had never opened a location there. We got to the point where the remodel was ready for fire marshal inspection when the tornado hit East Nashville on March 3rd. We couldn't get to our building and our neighborhood. Our neighbors were devastated by this tornado. This flowed straight into the coronavirus pandemic's onset, two weeks after the tornado. That was kind of D-Day for us. That was the day that restaurants started closing. It was the vicious cycle of last month's finances meeting this month's lack of income. And this wonderful, beautiful company that we built up to 290 people, crashed down on us. We were trying to figure out how to keep the 45 of us that were left after furloughs and closed dining rooms. There were 45 of us fighting like hell to figure out how to keep these buildings open by turning our restaurants into grocery stores. Lots of tears, then lots of grittiness. We relied on all the values of the company and remained creative, and we listened to our customers and what they needed. We made quick decisions.

Our loyal customer base rewarded us. Quick decisions rewarded us. And we're very happy to say that we've not only made it through, but we're a company three times stronger than we were before. We've opened our first out-of-state location since then. We're up to 342 employees, seven locations open, and the eighth one, Knoxville, getting close. We've also just announced location number nine for 2023, which will be the second one in Birmingham. This will be our first time opening three locations in a twelve-month period.

So, what is your daily work like today?

The types of things I'm doing are different, but it's not too different. I'm still running a tape measure. I'm still managing some of our highest relationships of banking and finance. I don't take three outfits anymore. I've matured into not caring as much. It's a complex and beautiful balance when your responsibility continually increases, but so does your flexibility as you get more people and more talented people involved. We now have a director of restaurants who runs the restaurants who's about to have her 10th anniversary with our company. My partner, who's our executive chef, just had his ten-year anniversary with the company. We've got an infrastructure of people who are way better at what they do than I am at their jobs.

There are times when everything's just running, and I'm thinking, "What do they need me for? What am I supposed to be doing right now?"

Chapter 18

Holly Rachel and Lena Winfree

Holly Rachel and Lena Winfree are co-founders of Rachel + Winfree Consulting, a data analytics consulting firm that provides data strategy consulting to small and medium businesses. After earning a Master of Science in Chemistry, Holly Rachel worked as a forensic scientist for the Tennessee Bureau of Investigation. Lena Winfree studied Health Science and Food Science in graduate school. She worked for more than twelve years at Meharry Medical School in Nashville as a research associate and data science manager. What initially brought them together as entrepreneurs were not based on either of their professional careers but on the side gigs each of them was pursuing.

Lena: It's a weird story, but we met each other at church. And Holly and I were doing very different side businesses at the time. She was working on a blog for haircare, and I was formulating hair products.

I introduced myself on Facebook. I said, "I thought it would be probably nice to partner because we are kind of the same interests in, you know, hair care. What do you think?"

Holly: I was in graduate school at the time. I never wanted to start a business, which is an interesting thing. My mom is an entrepreneur. She has her own therapy practice. Lena's mom was an entrepreneur, so we both came from an entrepreneurial background. We saw it in action. But I wanted to go to work, get my check, and come home.

When Lena proposed the idea, I was like, okay, I could do it in my spare time. She's making products. I was kind of mixing some stuff up and writing about different things I tried. So, we decided let's get together and see what we can do. That was our first business. We were buying ingredients and mixing up products in the kitchen. We came up with quite a few good ones. I was a chemist at the time studying infectious diseases at Vanderbilt.

Lena: I had moved over to Meharry right after we started. I was in the lab the whole time. It was like second nature for us to get into our kitchen and make it a laboratory. We were serious about it, and the product was great. People are still asking for it now.

Holly: I still use it.

Lena: To me it was a side hustle. I wasn't trying to make this a full-time thing. I was like, let's see where this goes. And we had a couple salons that were interested in our product, and it was going well. But we both knew we were going to be in the fields we were in. I don't even think we thought about that as a full-time thing at the time. I think that we had a lot to learn about entrepreneurship. And I remember one of our friends who was an entrepreneur. He said, "Just start! Just sell it." And we were like, "We don't have the right labels. It's not perfect." But he said, "Trust me, just sell it." But we did not just sell it. We knew we needed more capital in order to make it perfect.

Holly: At that point, we were both working full-time jobs. I was working at the Tennessee Bureau of Investigation. I was in the forensic sciences lab. One day I was talking to a defense attorney. He said, "My gosh, I love how you explain this. It's so clear. This is the most I've ever understood about what you all sent me. You know, I wish that I could have you guys come out to my firm and talk to all of us. I would pay for it!"

I went to my supervisor and said, "Hey, these defense attorneys would pay us to come out here and tell them what we do, how it works, and what it means when their client has five micrograms of diazepam. Nobody knows what that means."

He said, "No, we don't do that."

And I was like, "What do you mean? I'm giving you a whole other stream of income for the lab. You could simply send out your lab techs and not pay us anymore. Defense attorneys would pay you. They would pay the lab."

He said, "No, we don't do that."

I got home, called Lena, and said, "Girl, people will pay us to just tell them lab results. I think we should start a consulting company. This is how we can get money for our hair care business!"

So, that's when we started Rachel and Winfree Consulting. We were thinking we were going to get some quick money and put it into our haircare business. It's interesting how things kind of just start getting bigger and bigger. We realized a lot of people don't know their data.

Lena: Everybody keeps making it seem like data analytics is a new thing. It's not. It's the same data analysis that we were doing in the lab. I created interoperability between Nashville General and Meharry Medical College so that everybody can have one platform and share data. The "37208" information initially came from Nashville, Tennessee, when they found that we had the highest percentage of people incarcerated. We also found we had the highest rate of hypertension from that data set. People just don't understand their data. They don't even know what to do with it or how to use it. I was going from the dentistry department to pharmacology to all the different departments, explaining to them what they could do with their data and how to use it for their projects.

I was like, "You know what? Businesses need this. They need a data strategy. We should go and do this."

And so, we added that to our consulting, and the rest is history. It started off being a hobby for me. We didn't realize that this would take us to where we are now with being able to help make serious changes for people, communities, and companies just from knowing data and understanding it. It's been a very interesting journey to where we are now.

Holly: When we started Rachel and Winfree, we had about five different topics we were consulting on. And then we figured out people don't believe you can do all those things. Lena did the Data Science Institute at Meharry. She said, "Data is getting big. They're starting to talk about it. And small businesses don't know about this. But Google, Twitter, and everybody else are making so much money from analytics. Maybe we should just focus on that."

I was very worried about that because I did not know anything about analytics for business. But we realized, well, we could see a train coming down toward us. We can either get on, or we could miss it. So, we decided to focus on analytics. We started with that in 2019 when nobody was talking about data strategy for small businesses. We were definitely early, which made it a little bit harder because we didn't know how to navigate.

Lena: We've been able to do a lot for our community just by using data and showing people how to use their data. We've been able to help make businesses run better. Being black women to get this far and push the envelope for individuals who look like us to be taken seriously in this industry and environment is a huge undertaking.

Holly: The fact that this is hard, and this is why we do everything together because we aren't going to find the same working relationship in anybody else. We definitely talk to each other more than we talk to our spouses. We think it is absolutely a marriage.

Lena: And let me tell you, it was interesting because it just happened overnight. We came together out of respect and a mutual understanding that this is something we want to do in terms of business. I don't know if that is the reason why it has cultivated into a friendship/partnership that's lasted so long. In the beginning, we didn't know each other. Then come to find out, years later, it's one of the best relationships I think I've ever had in my life. We don't always agree. But we're able to move past those disagreements very easily.

I feel like we're yin and yang. I'm the one with the grandiose ideas about what we could be. And Holly keeps me very much grounded. Let's think about this in a logical way. How logistically could we do this? We balance each other.

Holly: We've learned that over time. Lena can read people very well, but she doesn't have a good feeling about whether it will work out. I don't have a problem trying something. We do something different, and sometimes it's okay. Maybe we'll go Lena's way, maybe we'll go Holly's way, or maybe we'll figure out a different solution.

Lena: You don't need anything but yourself. You're good enough. You don't need anything or anybody else to tell us what we can and cannot do. Entrepreneurs, we sometimes lack the confidence to know that we're enough and that what we have to offer is different from anybody else. So if we just kind of rest in that and do what we do well, it will come. And I know that it doesn't come overnight, even though that's what everybody makes it seem like. How many times have you seen these crazy Instagram posts? "We went from zero to $150,000!" Okay, but that took you five years. You may have done that, but don't make people think you did it overnight. The truth is it took time.

The journey of a woman who is black in America trying to do a business, you're going to get stressed out. They're going to tell you you're terrible. They're going to tell you you're not good enough. They're going to say to your face, "Why do you think you can do this?" They're going to say bad things to you. You're going to get spit on. You're going to get hurt. You're going to get these things. But I feel like it's still worth doing what you want and being that beacon of light based on what you can bring to your work.

Chapter 19

Grace Moore

When Grace was in college, she knew she wanted to do something entrepreneurial. At first, she thought she would launch an online women's clothing boutique. However, Grace realized that she could not achieve the mission and vision she had for her life through that particular concept. After college, she worked as a freelance graphic designer. Eventually, she found her entrepreneurial path with childhood friend and co-founder Maggie Brown through their startup, Recess Pickleball.

It is my life's mission to help more people have more fun. I have always found it so fulfilling to help people have a good time.

I was always kicking around business ideas. Even as a child, I was an entrepreneur. I had a candy stand at our neighborhood pool every summer where I would sit for hours selling candy to neighbors and friends. After college, I reconnected with one of my childhood friends, Maggie, who's now my co-founder. We both had an entrepreneurial zest and were excited about this idea of building a brand together. We were always tossing ideas back and forth.

During COVID, we both played a lot of pickleball. We couldn't find a single pickleball paddle that looked good. Everything was black and neon with dragons and volcanoes on it. We wanted to play with gear that matched our lifestyle and aesthetic.

We talked to other friends around the country who had also picked up pickleball during quarantine, so it seemed like a trend that was gaining a lot of steam. Thankfully, we both made a little money on the real estate boom in Austin, so we had some extra capital to invest in a new business. We quit our jobs and made it happen. It definitely is a right time, right place situation.

During COVID, people spent more time with family, and pickleball surfaced as a major trend. My husband and I loved the game. It allowed us to be outdoors, move our bodies, and be social and at a safe distance, which was crucial at that time. People all over the country got hooked and fell in love with pickleball.

Maggie had the idea for Recess. She was like, " I have a product that people will love. Will you help me bring the brand to life? Can you give it some color? We need a logo, a website, designs for the paddles, and social media!" I loved the idea right away. I love all things customer-facing. She took the lead on all operations, fulfillment, sourcing, and logistics, while I took the lead on design and social. We are a pretty good duo. We have our lanes and run full speed. Thankfully, we have a similar vision for what the brand should be, which makes it easy and fun.

We had the idea of targeting the recreational player. We set out to design gear that was as fun and approachable as the game itself. We want to grow with the player. A lot of these players are new to pickleball and are very recreational. But as they play more and grow with the game, we have plans to do the same. We want to be the premier pickleball brand. We are striving to have everything a player needs to get started and keep going with pickleball.

We partner with an incredible overseas manufacturer. We quickly learned that there is demand for custom pickleball paddles with a short turnaround time. To meet this demand, we opened a manufacturing site in Austin where we make custom pickleball paddles at our facility, which is really fun. Direct-to-consumer manufacturing is still currently based overseas because it still works so well. But now we can do smaller order quantities at our manufacturing site in Austin, which customers love. We currently have a MOQ of 25 with plans to lower it soon.[16] A lot of brands, such as J. Crew and Anthropologie, reach out to collaborate with Recess on custom pickleball paddles.

I think that quick execution has been our secret sauce. Mark Cuban says, "Perfect is the enemy of profit." That really inspired me. I'm a designer, so it's easy for me to get stuck trying to make something look perfect. But we have a short window of opportunity to get it out the door. We try a lot of different things and just let it evolve.

***

We had a good friend here in Austin we met while playing pickleball. He was like, "Oh my gosh, I love what you guys are doing. I would love to help you if you ever need to raise money."

And we said, "You know what? This is really working well. We have a

---

[16] Minimum Order Quantity

short window of opportunity to make it happen. And if we don't do it first, another company will. So, let's raise some money, maximize the window, and execute it really well."

A lot of VCs were interested in investing in the fastest-growing sport in the nation, thankfully. They were ready to talk with Recess. We were the first brand to the market with this kind of a design-forward, lifestyle approach to pickleball.

We partnered with a VC based in LA in 2022. We closed the deal the same week that I gave birth to my youngest son Arthur, which was really wild timing looking back.

Balancing my career, motherhood, marriage, a social life, and my mental/physical health is a big learning curve. It is only possible because I have such an amazing support system. My husband is my #1 cheerleader. My business partner is very family-focused herself and super respectful of my priorities and boundaries.

Phillip[17] is very understanding. Whenever I say, "Hey, I am hosting a pickleball tournament all day Saturday. I need to be there to run it and build brand awareness for Recess. Do you mind hanging with the kids all day?" And he's like, "Yes, absolutely. Hundred percent! We'll come hang out and bring lunch to the team." He's a remarkable partner, friend, and parent.

***

Whenever I pass by a pickleball court and I see Recess Paddles everywhere, it's a really crazy feeling. I still can't believe it. I am so thankful for the customers that resonate with the brand and choose to play with Recess paddles. It is a privilege to help people play and have fun.

I am really thankful for mentors who have helped me along the way. In general, I have learned that people are really open and willing to share their experiences. I don't even know how many times I have said "Hey, I don't know how to do this. How did you figure it out?" People are so quick to help or point you in the direction of someone they know who will help. It has made me want to pass along anything I have learned to other entrepreneurs and creatives in their journey.

[17] Phillip is Grace's husband. He is a product manager at Brightside.

ENTREPRENEURIAL VOICES

Chapter 20

Skylar Faria

Skylar Faria's father instilled in him a strong work ethic. His father put him to work at 13, working on farms in Southern California. Skylar also played baseball from a young age. He always dreamed of becoming a professional baseball player. After playing in junior college for two years, he made the team at California Polytechnic University, where the team earned two College World Series bids, winning one and coming in second in the other. He was signed by the Milwaukee Brewers to play minor league ball in the Pioneer League.

Skylar was successfully moving through his first season of minor league ball. And then, his vision changed. He became nearsighted. There were no corrective vision options that would work for him other than sports glasses. "I got in the box with the glasses on. I took one pitch, and I stepped out of the box, went to the dugout, left everything there, and drove home. Frustration over not being able to visually pick up the ball led to this being the end of a childhood dream.

Skylar took a job at Nordstrom as he finished up his degree at Cal Poly.

I'm working at Nordstrom. I was selling a pair of shoes, and a guy walked in with a 1980 College Baseball D-II World Series ring on. I was a part of the '83 & '85 world champion and runner up teams. He was older than I was. His name was Lance. I never knew him, but we kind of had that fraternal connection.

He said, "What are you doing here?"

And I said, "Well, hopefully, you'll buy a pair of shoes." He was looking at a $240 pair of Allen Edmonds dress shoes. And I said, "What do you do?"

And he said, "I sell sandpaper. Skyler, there's a position open in Southern California. You need to take it. We're hiring, and you would be perfect for the position. It's not like little paint stores and hardware stores. It is big manufacturers. As a matter of fact, I sold sandpaper to Louisville Slugger. They all use sandpaper for their bats. Are you sure you don't want to interview?"

He had mentioned that you get a company car, and I said, "Do I have to buy that car?" He said, "No, no, the company provides it."

And at that time, I drove an older model truck. I said, "Okay, let's go through the interview!" Crazy how a new vehicle can swing a decision.

I went through that interview, and during the entire interview with the national sales manager, all we talked about was baseball. And he said, Skyler, we'd like to bring you on board. I'll call you in a week.

I was tasked with first visiting small to midsize cabinet shops. I had no training. I pulled up in this Chevy Euro sport and walked into this shop wearing a sports jacket with a tie. And these two guys are in the back corner of the shop. One was over a table saw. They yell, "What do you want? Are you selling something?"

I said, "Yes, sir, I am."

And the one guy yells back at me, "I'm going to give you three orders today." I was like, damn, this is easy. Then he yelled, "We don't know who you are. So, get out, stay out, and don't ever come back."

I soon figured out that long-term residual income would come from developing relationships. And I knew that building trust was going to take time. I quickly learned that I had to stop selling and start listening.

I was with that company for 12 years. I had a territory of $3 million in sales. A lot of my customers started saying, "Skyler, can you get us personal protection equipment? Can you get me face masks? Can you get me wiping rags?"

And I said, "No, I can't."

I had developed building blocks of trust over the 12-year period, thus the reason my customers began asking for product support aside of the abrasives I supplied them with leading me to resigning and venturing off with my own business.

And so, I ended up resigning, and I started my own business.

At that time, Meri and I had gotten married. She was finishing up her college at San Luis Obispo. I faxed my resignation, and I didn't tell her. Right. And I knew I didn't. I didn't tell her.

With the commission plan I had with my employer, I made too much money. I was grossing almost 180 grand a year. And that became a problem for management there because another guy and I were making more than even the CEO.

Everything I did from the age of seven was play sports, baseball, football, and basketball. There were goal lines in football, bases with home plate in baseball, and hoops in basketball for a reason. There were no participation trophies. To "win the game" you have got to score a run, cross the goal line or make that shot to win the game. I treated serving customers like being in and playing the game, a game in which the goal was to win.

As a partner supplier, it's your job to teach about the features and benefits of your products. But none of this matters until you get in front of the owner of a company who's struggling and bleeding. The real part of it is when the person who's bleeding, the owner or the plant manager of a factory, is gushing excessive material costs or labor costs though a "massive pipe" out the back of a his/her building. And unless you can "cauterize the wound," you're of no value to them by simply slapping a "band-aid" on it by cutting pricing, etc.

I was concerned but not over worried with having a guaranteed paycheck. The next month I didn't have a paycheck. Then Meri comes home, and she's like, "Wow, what are you going to do?"

I'm like, "I'll figure it out."

It was similar to being back in Montgomery, Alabama in the college baseball world series. Bases are loaded. You've got no balls and two strikes. And what I'm thinking is I've got to perform. I've got to see the ball hit the sweet spot on the barrel of a bat. And I need to drive that ball right through the throat of the pitcher and "pin it against the fence!" You know life isn't easy. And when you're in the game, you're in that moment. You're either the hero or you're forgotten. So, when I left, I knew I had a solid group of customers that trusted me. And all I needed to do was surround myself with good vendors/manufacturers, so I had the products or systems to help these people.

The customers were telling me where they wanted me to be. To get to that spot, you must understand their processes, how they do things, and the results they're expecting. And then you have to understand your competition. You need to understand where they stand in the market. And then you just carve your way through there and make it happen. My biggest competitor was the six inches between my ears. Negative self-talk shuts the doors in the minds of young entrepreneurs leading to unfulfilled dreams and goals.

In December of 2003, Marina, the wife of the owner of my biggest vendor, called me and said, "I'm selling the business today. I've called you first, you and Meri, and I need an answer by 5:00 today if there's an interest in purchasing the company." An unfortunate death in the family lead to her decision in selling the company.

That threw me in a tailspin because this is a multimillion-dollar company. I didn't know how to do this, but they were a critical vendor to me. I had become their friend, and I knew then why she had reached out to us. It was because of the connection and relationship. And so, what she decided to do was sell us the company and carry back the loan. At that time, she had a two-month-old baby girl. We did not want to buy the company, and she wanted nothing to do with the company. We got the company for much less than what it could have been sold for.

She came back to Meri and me exactly a year later, at our Christmas party, and said, "I made a mistake. And I'm not sure if you would agree or not, but considering the conditions that I was in, I could have gotten X number of dollars more."

I looked at Marina and said, "I agree with you 100%."

And she said, "Well, I'd like to buy the company back."

Meri and I said no.

I went to every person I knew, both sets of our parents, other businesspeople we knew, friends, and family, and I said, "What would you all do?" And the final consensus was, a deal's a deal. Business is business.

We got back to Marina and said, "We're going to give you, to the exact penny, what you're asking for additionally. We will do this over the next five years without any interest."

Marina is still one of Meri's dearest friends today. Her daughter, Nicole, just graduated from college. We've always believed in doing the right thing. And we're blessed beyond measure. And it's been one hell of a ride.

Her father, George Dixon, invented the drywall sanding block. So, I had these basic products and knew that so much more could be done with them. And it started me on this journey of creating and developing different products. In 2015, we were awarded the highest award in the industry, referred to as the Visionary Award. It is awarded based on innovation, creativity, and productivity. We have companies that use the SurfPrep sanding system to complete the circle in the Lean manufacturing for their Six Sigma or their Kaizen black belt.

***

I was in North Carolina, in the Hickory area, at Stickley furniture. I was with the sales rep for the cabinet hardware distributor named Michelle. She said, "Now, Skylar, a lot of these people down here in the South, they don't like people from California or New York. And I will tell you, they don't like being sold."

I don't remember this lady's name. She was on the end of a finishing line. She had been standing in the same room for 27 years, sanding chairs. This woman looked like a million dollars. She looked like she had just gotten out of church. And this lady took the sanding system. Michelle looked at me and said, "She has never done this with anything I brought in here." She threw her arms in the air, and she started hollering at Michelle. She's like, "Lord Jesus, Michelle, who is this man again from California? I have never had a sanding system like this in my life. My hand don't hurt. My wrist don't hurt."

***

This journey has been amazing and a blessing. My role has been one of a visionary where Meri's been the integrator, balancing out one another in the organization. We both work a combined 120 hours per week easily and now are putting together our exit strategy.

All three of our kids are in the business now. We have 29 employees. Our employees played a role in being a part of hiring our kids. I did the same thing my dad did to me with the kids. They were unloading containers at the age of seven or eight. They're solid humans. They're all married. We're in the heat of trying to sort through whether they will buy the company back from us. The big thing for us is the culture and our core values. We live by our core values. Our employees are like family. As a group, we created core values. I said, "I want these core values to be applicable to you and your own family. So how do you want your children to respond to you when you give them directions?" The result is, how many people have you helped and encouraged in life? How many people have you helped? How many people have you impacted in life? That's really it.

Meri and I just went through a life altering event with some of our closest friends where the wife suddenly passed due to an incurable cancer. This friend was in the delivery room with Meri when our daughter Hannah was born. Meri was in the delivery room when her friend gave birth to her daughter, one of Hannah's closest friends. Life can be unkind. Our friend just retired from teaching at the age of 56. Her husband is highly successful with his own business in the state of California. They had it all. And then, in late September 2022 that diagnosis came in with stomach cancer changing the course of all our lives forever. We were at her celebration of life at the end of October. Our long time pastor and friend shared a story at this celebration of life where it's not your birth date and passing date that matters, but more so what kind of life did you live while here on earth. How many people benefitted by your love and time you invested in them? It's "the dash" or time period you were alive where you actively demonstrated serving others unconditionally without any expectation for anything in return. That's the life I work daily on living, just like our loving friend.

Chapter 21

Gordon Droitcor

Gordon started out his career in the audio side of the music business. He got started by recording bands in junior high. This led him to study audio engineering in college. However, the reality of making a living in audio engineering was not what Gordon had envisioned. Eventually, this led him down an entirely different direction in his career.

After college, I went on the road with some pretty large artists as the stage audio guy, which was the one that helped to handle all the microphones, the in-ear monitors and all of the RF wireless stuff on stage. You also help the opening act band get their sound going. These opening act guys, even though they weren't headlining, they're still playing for 15,000, 20,000, 30,000 people because the real show was 60,000. But at the time, these artists didn't have any production. They had a couple of risers and their instruments, and that was it. I was looking at this massive rig that they weren't using. I would become friends with these opening act bands and their management over time.

I'd ask, "Why don't you do more production?"

"Well, it's just too expensive. We can't afford it."

And I'd ask, "Is the gear expensive?

"No. The gear is acceptable. A lot of times we get it for free because it's already there. It's the people who run it: that is expensive."

At this time, I was getting a little bit worn out by audio and touring. This is where I kind of had a major, very clear "aha" moment. I said, I know I do audio, but I'm around these lighting people and know enough about it to be dangerous. I realized that there is a way to use the audio software almost all bands already use, to trigger lighting and video cues. This can eliminate some of these expensive people. I think that can work.

Most bands have a piece of software that plays their backing tracks. It's like having an extra band member on stage to play the instrumentation that you don't have a person for. This might be a beat, a vocalist line, or a violin line. You put that into software called Ableton, which is a software that plays back the tracks. But everyone uses that for audio only. I realized that this software gave you the ability to layout MIDI triggers, which are primarily made for audio. These MIDI triggers sent "go" messages to different pieces of software and hardware to make them react automatically. I also found out that the lighting software also accepts these triggers. Instead of it triggering musical notes, you can make it trigger a lighting console and say, "Kick, snare, flash, flash, flash" the lights. And so, we just connected those two things, and it removed such a highly skilled person out front triggering the lighting. Because at the end of the day, they're just doing it to the music anyway. It is automated this way and it gets locked in. Honestly, some of this was used already at the arena level, but no one wanted to focus on a solution for these smaller bands.

So, I tried it and built it and then pitched a band on using it. I told them that I'm sending them on the road with a lighting rig that's completely automated and they don't need an extra person to run it.

They said, "It sounds dangerous."

I told them it probably is. I don't know if this is going to work or not, but they don't have to pay me to do it.

We were the outsiders. We weren't coming from the lighting world, doing it the old "lighting way." I was coming from the audio world and my business partner, Erik, was a tour manager.

I remember when I first started doing this asking some people to borrow some of their lights so I could learn how to do it. And they said in a half joking manner, "I'll let you borrow the lights, but just don't compete with me or take my bands." But we got so many artists because we were the only ones doing it. And then that's when we heard, "You're taking all the groups and you're doing it in the way that we don't like." We were hated in the traditional touring lighting world.

So, we were two guys coming into the lighting world from the outside: no clue what we were doing. But our whole thing was that we weren't designers. We're a solution. The arrangement of lights wasn't the main selling point in our eyes. It's just like a layout that happened to work with the lights that the vendor had. Then, we started talking to the vendors. These are the shops that rent the equipment to tours.

We'd say, "What's collecting dust? We'll make a design with that."

And then we would then design something, put it into a safe layout, program it, and then put it on the road. You can build all the lights on a rack and then not have to assemble it every day. How do you roll it in the place, plug it in and be done? How do you make it as easy as possible, because there's non-lighting people setting this up, like tour managers and even the band.

We got Erik's dad to scrounge up some cash and loan it to us to build set carts that we would rent out to these groups. We made some really horrible decisions on those first carts in how they were designed. We spent a bunch of money on getting them made and then used it for that tour and then later realized that it was too specific of a layout. We can't use it again. So, we learned the hard way! We perfected our setcart design and got new ones made. And then we made it easier and easier for these groups to put stuff on.

But what was happening was a dilemma. It was a dilemma of us making business decisions that we thought was what people wanted. But the reality was, they wanted something else. We wanted to make that thing because it was a cool tool, not that it was the right creative answer. What we were doing was making more and more of these set carts and a lot of rinse, repeat, design ideas. What the artist really wanted was boutique shit that nobody else offered. We thought we could get away with three designs for every band. We thought that's what people would like. Managers liked that because it was financially responsible. Artists were like, "No!" And so, we ended up becoming a design firm by accident because we needed to design boutique stuff every time. We thought we should hire somebody who knows how to do that, but all of them were crazy expensive. So, we learned how to design lighting. We shifted from "solutions" to create a boutique design firm.

It was really hard. We had to make our pitches look pretty, which means more software and better computers. It put us into a new tier. It was harder, but we could charge more because of that. There was a lot of not knowing what we were doing and just making big mistakes. You send a tour out with a certain software, and then somebody really smart says you could use this software instead. We just grew by accident.

Lighting design then naturally evolved into a set design, which means lighting plus the staging layout. Then that naturally moved into designing the video layout, like projection and video screens. And then that led into animating the content for set screens. There was a natural evolution of walking down a path and then you're like, "Well, we're paying those other things, outsourcing all this other stuff, and it's not that great quality-wise. Hell, we can take a crack at that." And then we just started a little capillary off of our main vein. And so, that's how we got to where we are now is by doing the stuff that made sense to do in-house. This was the departure from working only with smaller bands and now we were working with household name artists.

Erik and I worked our tails off in 2019, and it was our most profitable year. But it was the most crushing timewise. We were just dead. We did 30 big tours, and it was just nuts. At that moment, we didn't realize that this wasn't sustainable. And so, at the time, we weren't even smart enough to really realize we needed to do something else.

COVID was equally the most devastating thing that happened to our business, but also the most needed thing to happen to our careers. It was devastating in the fact that touring completely shut down our income stream -- went to zero. We used our reserves to keep our staff on full pay. Erik and I didn't pay ourselves for a full year. We lived off our own savings and just squeezed by. That was dark as it gets for us.

But during that time, the enlightening part was we had other ideas for other businesses.

One of which started off as an answer to COVID but ended up being something that is actually a really viable business regardless of COVID. We were looking at like the Christmas experience market and that was this idea that you could drive through this Christmas display. What if we did that using our tour design experience to make a drive thru visual experience? Erik said, "Ooh, I'm gonna do that." And so, he went off down the rabbit hole of figuring out how to do it and pulled off an incredible show.

Even before COVID, I had this concept of a physical product, which is now a product that I'm working on. The idea started out while I was sitting listening to vinyl in my home. The feeling of walking up to the record player, pulling the vinyl out, and putting it on the record player. And then you take the album cover and lean it up against the speaker; it was all part of the listening experience. But then after four songs, you have to flip the record or change it. That was cumbersome and made me want to stop using it. I wish I could just turn on a playlist, but also see the visual side. And as I said that, I had my third "aha" moment of my life, which was what is now called Syne. It is the idea of having a companion display that connects with how you stream music to show you all of the stuff of vinyl or have it give you the feeling of vinyl. The tagline is "the feeling of vinyl in a streaming world." It's the comfort of analog with the convenience of digital. There wasn't a solution out there for it.

So, I called the only software programmer I knew to get it going!

"I have an iPad. Can you make me an app that just shows me album artwork "big?"

It was in a browser: it wasn't that sexy. But I found myself not turning it off. I used it all the time. People would come over (this is still before COVID) and they're like, "What is that? What happens? Can I have it?" I put them on the test flight and let them have it. I had six people using it and they all said, "This is awesome. This is so great. You should do this!"

I started to moonlight this a bit because I thought it was pretty interesting. And then COVID hit. I brought it up to Erik and said, "I think I really want to do it. I want to bring it into Cour Design and make it my thing." And he just was like, "Holy shit! That's a good idea. All right, we're in it together now."

But if you look at all of these, Cour Design, Cour Content, Syne, EAMOTION, all of them are just music and aesthetics. It is the connection of sound and visual. And that's what we've been doing this whole time. It's just eyes where your ears are. It's all about the connection of those things and how they work together. That's what we really care about. And that's what I'm working on now.

Chapter 22

Josh Gilreath

Josh Gilreath had always known he wanted to be an entrepreneur. In high school, he started his first business in photography. He learned from his uncle, a well-known photographer in his hometown. Significant technological innovations in photography led to major disruptions, which left his business model behind. He then moved into construction, a business his parents had been in for many years. He had some success, but his heart was never really in the business. About the time he was ready to get out of construction, a few random and unplanned events eventually led him to start his catering business called Tennessee Rebel BBQ.

I got to where I dreaded waking up every morning and seeing what phone calls I had missed and what emails remained in my inbox. Commercial construction is a very high-stress industry. We ultimately kind of just fizzled out.

That's when I got reacquainted with smoking meats. It was kind of a fluke. I was in Chattanooga at my parent's house one weekend. It was early summer. They were about to run out to the Walmart to buy some pool chemicals and then come back for an afternoon around the pool. I went along.

Well, the pool chemicals at Walmart are near the garden center. My mom immediately starts looking at all the flowers. Me and my dad walked around "kicking the tires" on all the grills and the smokers. And I was just like, "I would like to get a smoker. I'd kind of like to monkey around with that. I think that would be kind of fun."

The smokers were all $300 to $500. That seemed like a little bit of an investment for a weekend project. I turned the corner, and there were two little smokers. I didn't know enough about smokers at the time to tell the difference, but they were different. They looked the same because they were little charcoal bullet smokers. They were both marked at 35 bucks. And I was like, "Okay, I can throw away $35 and a bag of charcoal. We can see if this is going to be fun."

I ended up taking the one that had the paperwork in it and looked like a more complete kit. When I got home, I found out it was a $220 Weber smoker they had mismarked for the same price as the cheaper version made by Walmart. So, I got a really nice smoker for almost nothing. I fired it up that afternoon. It was the first rack of ribs I ever did. They were nothing to win an award with, but I enjoyed the process, so I kept at it. I kept monkeying around. I think everything we ate we smoked! Finally, I started to dial it in and get the hang of it.

As I got more proficient in cooking the meat, I got tired of having to go to the store and buy the commercially made spice rubs and blends. I monkeyed around and came up with my own. And I'm like, "Ha! Okay, here's the business. I can bottle and sell the spice rub. That's where it all started.

I toyed with the idea of selling my rub but also kept cooking. And then, I had some people start asking me, "Hey, could you smoke this for me? And I'll pay you."

So I started doing that a little bit here and there, and I got to thinking. I'm like, "Wait a minute, I don't want to sell my rub. That's my secret! I want to do the whole package. But how do I go about doing the whole package? I have literally zero experience in the food service industry."

I applied for a job at Green Hills Grille in Green Hills waiting tables. I took out my resume, and they're like, "You started a photography business. You owned a couple of different construction companies. What in the world do you want with waiting tables?"

I said point blank, "Look, I think that I want to have a food business. I don't have any experience in the business. So, I want to start from the ground up and see what there is to learn."

I worked there for almost a year. I got an offer from a friend in the industry to come to another restaurant that would give me bartending and front-of-house management experience.

I was starting to get a little more going with the barbecue. I was like, "Okay, maybe now's time to go full-time about it." That happened mid-late summer, so I kind of got a late start that year. I didn't have the momentum to really get ready to go. Things had flattened out again. I needed to make some money.

So, I went back into working in a restaurant as a full-time bartender. I worked literally every day until March 15th, 2020. The manager comes through and says, "I think we might be closing early today because we're not busy, and there's something going on about this whole coronavirus thing. We're not really sure. We're waiting to hear back from corporate and make a call as to what we're going to do."

We shut it down, and they promised we'd only be closed until that coming Tuesday. They did reopen, but it wasn't until May, so I never went back.

That was the time when it's like, okay, I don't have a choice. We've got to kick this barbecue thing in the ass and figure out what the hell we're going to do. It was a bonus having lost my job because the unemployment benefits helped bridge that gap for a couple of months and allowed me the freedom to figure out what we needed to do.

We had a 14-foot box trailer left over from doing construction. I upgraded my smoker from the original little one. Unfortunately, my box trailer and car were stolen. We had a cousin down in Florida who passed away. She had never married and never had kids. Her entire estate went to all of the cousins. When my dad got his first part of the settlement, he said, "I want to take this, and let's get the tools we need, and let's kick this business in the ass."

We were able to buy the 28-foot trailer we have now, which is massive. Bought a smoker that is about 1600 pounds. It's on a trailer itself and pulls up into the big trailer. That really upped our game and made it to where it's no problem to cook for a couple hundred people now. We got it all stickered up with our logo and everything, which is the only money that we have spent on any kind of advertising thus far. And I think it was probably the best dollars we could have spent. I can't go anywhere without somebody stopping and asking questions. We're not a food truck. We just use the trailer to haul our equipment and then cook on-site. Whenever we go to a fall festival or a barbecue competition, we've got the biggest rig on the lot and it's just plastered with our name. People notice.

I got a phone call asking about catering. They asked if we could do stuff on-site and handle about 125 to maybe 175 people three Saturdays in June. A few days later, I got a phone call. It's Vanderbilt's football program. So we catered for their entire football team and all their recruits for the month of July when they were doing their summer recruiting camp. We did it on their practice field, so we literally pulled the trailer into the endzone, and they had tables and chairs on the football field.

Given the fact that we have the equipment and the capabilities to do what we can do, I'm looking for this year to be a fuller calendar than it was last year. I'd like to get to a point where I can bring on some additional help that would allow us to do more events. The next step after that is looking into renting some kitchen space or getting in with a commissary. That would be a crucial thing for us to have if we're going to try to scale up from what we're doing now.

I would love to have a restaurant at some point someday. That's maybe like a 10 or 15-year plan. I don't know yet. It's out there, but I haven't really put a ton of serious thought into how I want to get there yet because there are too many other little steps in the meantime.

Summer is obviously the busiest time of year. Usually, in March, when the weather starts to break and it starts to get a little nicer, that's when things ramp up. May gets busier. June and July are obviously slammed. And then you start getting into September and October with all the fall festivals. We pretty much stay busy up through Christmas. January is traditionally dead, and February is not much better.

In an effort to fill in the gaps, I have been able to partner with a local cigar shop in Chattanooga, TN, which is allowing us the ability to host "pop-up" events whenever we have a free weekend. This really kicked off in December of 2023 with our first event of cooking for the SEC Championship football game. Then, subsequently, we were invited back to cook for the National Championship game in January! We have several more dates on the calendar, which is really allowing us to start having a "regular" spot that we can promote like many of the more traditional food trucks do. In addition to a regular "pop-up" with the cigar shop, we have been formally invited back home to Belmont University to host a "pop-up" in the main dining hall in January of 2024. At the rate things seem to be "popping-up," we may not have to be too concerned with opening a brick-and-mortar restaurant but rather go to other people's places and "pop-up!"

Section 4

Youthful Exuberance

"The young do not know enough to be prudent, and therefore they attempt the impossible – and achieve it, generation after generation."
Pearl S. Buck

Chapter 23

Sarah Beth Perry

Sarah Beth's entrepreneurial aspirations were inspired by her dad and stepdad, who are both entrepreneurs. At a young age, Sarah Beth started a nonprofit, sold bracelets, set up lemonade stands, and so forth. She combined her entrepreneurial ambitions with her love for music during her college years, where she launched her business called "With the Band."

I was a huge music fan growing up. I remember seeing fans congregate and create these fan meetups and fan projects on a small level. As a fan, I wanted to be involved in them but didn't know how to get involved. When I was at Belmont University, I learned that the artists' teams were also having a problem with fan engagement. I saw this as a gap in the market.

Fan engagement is any type of communication you are having with the fan, whether that's a direct message to a fan or the overall marketing of a tour to a fan. Nielsen did a study that showed that 20% of fans generate over 70 to 80% of the total revenue. Your super fans are where the money lies. The purpose of fan engagement is to convert a person who just heard your name on the radio to someone who is spending money on your music and merchandise.

I didn't think much about it until my sophomore year. I was in the Foundations of Entrepreneurship class. Someone came in and told us about a business plan competition. The applications were due on Monday. One of my friends was in the class and I said to her, "I've had this idea, but I don't know if I should do it." She said, "You can't write a business plan in three days!"

But I ended up going to Fido[18] all weekend and wrote the business plan. When I made the pitch at the competition, it was the first time I had told more than five people about my idea. "With The Band" was an app where a fan could do everything in one place: see updated tour dates, talk to bands, and see information about multiple artists. I ended up winning the competition.

The MVP was an app/platform where fans could join or create different

---

[18] A local coffee shop in Nashville.

fan projects or fan meetups. I completely bootstrapped the startup. My intention was to create ten different marketing ideas and spend a little money on each one and see what works. And then keep doing whatever works.

We launched our own large fan project at the Jonas Brothers show. We did not ask anyone's permission to do anything. I think it cost us around like $800, which in the scheme of things is nothing compared to what it gave us. We created 16,000 signs that said, "Thank you for coming back to us." It was the Jonas Brothers' reunion tour. The signs had instructions for the fan to hold it up during the song "Comeback". To let fans know, we created a fan project group on our app. It also went on all the other social media channels. We ended up getting a group of ten fans together. Before the show, I gave them a clear bag full of 2,000 signs. We all went into the concert arena right when the doors opened. Everyone knew what section they were supposed to be putting the signs out. I actually had a broken foot at this time, so I had a boot on. We had no idea if it was going to work at all. I just remember hoping a few hundred people would hold them up. When the song came on. I felt the tension and wondered, "Is this going to work?"

And then all of a sudden, it was just like a sea of white and all you could see were the signs. And it was really cool, too. It was right after a break. So only one brother came on stage at a time. You got to see each of their individual reactions to it, which was cool. And by the end of it, all three of them were crying on stage. It ended up trending on Twitter for two days and it got a bunch of major press write-ups. That's when we realized that we had something really special. We can create such a special memory and moment that emotionally moves so many people.

That is then what morphed into the first revenue stream. Initially the app didn't have any monetization. But then, an artist or sponsors started to be willing to pay us to create these events at their shows. The Jonas Brothers team ended up reaching out to us, and so did other artists' teams because they saw what we had created.

I sent a cold email about creating an event at Kacey Musgraves's show. For her, we created a rainbow during the song "Rainbow". She had just won album of the year at the Grammys. For that one, depending on where the fan was sitting, they had a different color sheet of paper. On the back, it had instructions for them to hold it up to their phone flashlight. So that created this glowing sea of rainbow lights during the song.

And so that became our revenue stream. But then COVID hit. And so those events couldn't happen anymore.

While no shows were going on, we ended up developing our whole app and created the web platform, as well, to enable an artist to create their own Fan Crew. It is a modern-day version of a fan club. It's a turnkey solution that has zero startup costs for the artists. When a fan purchases a membership, 70% of the money goes directly to the artist. After we deal with random tech fees, we get whatever's left over of the 30%.

Why do the artists come to us? The main reason a larger artist needs us is because right now they don't have anywhere to manage their fanbase. They're using several different social media channels: Instagram, Facebook, Twitter, TikTok, whatever. On those channels they aren't getting any fan data, so they don't know a fan's email and they don't know exactly where they are. They can see large overall demographics, but they don't get any individual fan information. We can give them that. The second reason they need us is to make revenue. This was important during COVID. And the third reason they need us is to have a better connection with fans. Fans get to see a little bit of a different side, especially the more the artist is involved. Artists can actually hear the stories from the fans on what a song means to them. In one fan group we have a channel where all the fans are posting photos and talking about the show every night. They hear what their actual fanbase is talking about and what they enjoyed. They learn how to cater to their audience more.

With the Band helps fans meet other fans and create friendships. I met so many of my best friends in music and I just feel like music does have such a massive way of bringing people together. We get comments all the time like, "I met my best friend through y'all three months ago." I wanted to try to harness that power and be able to help artists do the same with their fanbases. And so, I always say I feel I will have been successful when there's a bunch of Fan Crews started and there are hundreds of artists on the platform.

Look ahead 40 or 50 years. What will your career have looked like?

A year ago, I don't think I would have told you that I'm eventually going to sell With the Band. But I think the longer I do it, the more I definitely cannot see myself keeping up with this pace the rest of my life. I used to think this would be my only company. I don't know why I really ever thought that in the first place. For so long I was so obsessed with music and thought I would only ever do music things. But in the past year, a lot has changed. I still love music and I still think I'll probably be involved with it in some aspects the rest of my life. But I think I will have done things inside and outside of music. I think I probably will be a lifelong entrepreneur. And I think success would really look like knowing when it's the right time to stop and do a different one. And with each venture, I'm gaining happiness.

I think one thing I struggle with about the whole entrepreneur thing, in general, is that there is such a mentality that to be a successful startup you have to fundraise. I don't understand why that's viewed as important. The whole plan of a startup is to make money. So, you should just try to get to revenue as quickly as possible. And so, I think the thing I would do differently next time I start a business is finding ways in the beginning to make the revenue so you can keep testing different hypotheses of, "Would people pay for this?"

I feel like a lot of times that the companies that I'm compared to are all businesses that have a lot of money invested in them. Most of their first rounds are over a million. And because they aren't bootstrapping and they aren't worried about every penny. They aren't seeing the ROI of every penny and what is most important to put the money toward. One company like ours raised $20 million the first round of funding never made a single dollar revenue. How can you put so much money into something and you never see one dollar in return? It is just stupid to me. I personally think they just didn't test their hypotheses and they just think people are going to spend money on something. I think in the long run, bootstrappers win.

I always say that I don't think I could be doing anything else: physically, mentally, all the above. I feel like entrepreneurship is probably one of the hardest paths to take. I just absolutely love that I get to learn so much and then create a process. Then I get to teach someone else how to do it, hand it off, and just keep learning new things. I think my favorite part about entrepreneurship is that I am naturally curious about a lot of things, and I get to explore new things on a daily basis. And so, today I'm learning Facebook advertising and then tomorrow I'm going to learn how to take photos for a photo shoot and how to work the camera. Learning a bunch of different skills, has definitely been my favorite part.

Chapter 24

Hannah Rodriguez

Hannah was just a child when she launched her business. I find it hard to imagine any of my children or grandchildren becoming an active entrepreneur at such a young age. And yet she did it!

When I was ten years old, I found my entrepreneurial spirit on YouTube talking about my American Girl Dolls. I would teach how to do their hair and how to take care of them. I even made stop-motion videos about them. YouTube was a new platform. My parents wouldn't let me show my face, which was smart. I'm thankful they let me start that channel because it's what catapulted my whole career.

I wasn't coming to it from the sense of like, "Oh, I need to make money. I need to make sure I'm promoting myself. I need to build a personal brand." I didn't even know that word yet: personal brand. I came at it from an authentic place of wanting to build a community of like-minded girls who also liked their dolls and wanted to talk about them and share. And I think that's why I've stuck with it for so long. I've had a love for content creation and community building instead of trying to take it from a business perspective.

I applied to be a part of YouTube AdSense. I had enough subscribers at the time, so I made a couple of cents. I was like, "Dang, this is amazing. I can buy myself another American Girl doll in a few months." So that was when I realized it could make some money. I saw girls who were older than me, not going to college and doing it full-time.

I kept with my YouTube channel throughout middle school, high school, and college. In high school, I started making videos about my lifestyle, productivity, and how I manage my routines, being a busy student while also being a YouTuber. It was a very natural transition. As you grow up, your interests change, your passions change. I was in high school when YouTube started getting really popular with the "beauty guru community." They were huge, with millions of subscribers sharing information about makeup tips and fashion.

And then, around my sophomore year of high school, around the age of sixteen, there was a term that went viral called "Girlboss." So, me being an aspiring "Girlboss," I made a morning routine video of the tips I'm seeing all these Forbes women doing in their morning routines. I'm doing it even though I'm in high school! I made a video about that, which went viral: millions of views. That helped me gain an older audience who was looking into the world of productivity and time management.

I didn't want my identity to be caught up in the number of followers or my sales. I tried to be really good about saying, "Okay, I have my own worth that's in me, that's in my face, that's in my family and values. And it's not tied to my business, who I am online, and how many people like my posts." Realizing that early on has been a huge help. And if I do get something negative that gets posted, I can block it out and be like, "That's okay. My worth isn't tied to that person's words."

I think it's more about knowing what to share and what not to share. I don't share a ton online about my family or my relationship with my boyfriend. I keep my content about myself because I signed up for this. I try to keep some things private for myself and for my relationships, and that's just the decision I've made. That's probably hindered my growth in some ways because it's usually the influencers or the TikTokers who share their whole lives online that get viral quickly. After all, people love that you're sharing everything. But for me, I just wanted to keep it separate.

I was getting bored in the fall of my freshman year in college. I needed something else to work on besides just YouTube and school. I remember curling my hair in my freshman year dorm, and I was thinking how cool it would be to have a physical product for my audience that correlates with the content they love: time management. So, I thought maybe some kind of planner where women my age who have similar goals, want to have all these extra side hustles, be a good student, and take care of themselves, can do it all in one place. So that is how I came up with the product, the Dream Achieve Workbook, which started my product-based business.

I had no idea what to do because I had only done content and service-based products. So, as most good entrepreneurs do, I went to Google and researched how to find a manufacturer. The majority of my freshman year I spent just researching and getting samples.

My first round of inventory cost about $3,000. I paid for it all out of pocket because I'd been making money throughout high school doing YouTube. I had the inventory shipped to my parent's house and drove three hours each way to get the inventory. I shipped it out to my customers from my dorm.

TikTok made me believe that people outside of people who know my name would want this product. In the summer of 2021, I had a few videos go viral on TikTok. I had millions of views and sold out of all the inventory I had left that summer within a week. It's been hard to replicate that. A few years ago, getting that virality from content was easy. Now you can post that same content, and it may not perform the same. That's just how it is. Social media changes monthly, weekly, so it's hard to replicate success. But that was a great way for me to see that this is something people who have no idea who I am are willing to spend the money on and purchase my product. Thanks to my YouTube and TikTok audiences, I've also been able to sell globally. We're in 50 countries.

I have two separate businesses: my personal brand, Hannah Ashton, and then my product company Dream Daily LLC. In the next ten years, I would love to build Dream Daily to function financially on its own. It's still a ways off. I still pay myself through my content creation through Hannah Ashton. Content creation is the way you make more money. I just have a passion for Dream Daily. I want to create products for driven young women that could help them achieve the goals that I've been able to achieve. It is tempting to just focus on content creation. But then I remember how much I love the business side of things. I want to be able to grow a team and build a workplace culture.

I've had a lot of days when I've not been sure about the business. More so since I graduated because you're no longer a student with that safety net under you. Paying all my own bills, paying for everything, is a lot of pressure. I want to show up every morning and be busy. It's deciding what work needs to get done that day versus another day and determining what's going to move the needle. I think that's the challenge for me these days. I want it to work, I want it to grow, but what exactly do I need to focus on today for it to grow? There have been a lot of days where I see my friends, who are in their 9 to 5 jobs, who can just show up and be told exactly what to do, get off at a certain time, and have guaranteed that paycheck. Meanwhile, I show up and am ready to go, but I don't always know what to do. And the paycheck isn't guaranteed.

I still work from home. I work by myself, which has its depressing moments when there's no one else to talk to about business decisions. Yeah, you can call a friend or call a parent, but they don't know the business like you do and what you're going through. It's very isolating.

I realized this summer when I had gone multiple days without seeing someone, that I needed to get outside of my apartment and see a friend, someone who knows me. Not just someone you meet at the grocery store or a barista, but get coffee and work from a coffee shop *with* someone else.

I'm hoping to bring on an intern in 2023. I think just having someone who I see on a regular basis to talk through the business and talk through goals and brainstorm with is going to be a tremendous help.

I like to have a start and end to my workday. I wake up, and before I start work, I journal. I have my coffee, read my Bible, and walk outside to get some sunlight before I'm in my apartment all day. And then, towards the end of the day, I'm ready to turn it off. I know a lot of entrepreneurs like work late into the night. I'm done by 5 or 6 p.m. Even though I love what I do, I'm ready to have my night routine and read, watch TV, talk to friends, or whatever. I'm trying to build those boundaries.

It's easy to compare where I am to other entrepreneurs. I turned twenty-three in October, and during that time, I was struggling. On my worst day, I told myself, "I am proud of you. You are paying for your apartment, a car, and your life, and you are doing this all on the businesses you have built. This actually is success."

I'm proud of myself for getting to this point!

Chapter 25

James Richard and Ethan Akdamar

James Richard and Ethan Akdamar met in Dallas right after graduating high school. Their friendship grew stronger when they went to the same college. Once at school, they both became entrepreneurship majors. While still in school, they started their business, initially named Vitamin Honey. They built enough momentum working on the business in college to grow the company together after graduation.

James: My younger brother has Crohn's disease. He was on a specific carbohydrate diet, which eliminates all polysaccharides, processed foods, and other ingredients. One of the only sweeteners he could use was honey. He was putting honey on everything. That got me thinking.

While he was on his diet, he had to take vitamins to help supplement his nutrition. I didn't realize that a lot of vitamins had all these extra fillers that he was avoiding in his diet. I was like, "Whoa, why don't we just eliminate those extra ingredients and put them into something tasty, like honey that he already uses?" That's how our business idea was born.

We were in class, and I asked Ethan if he wanted to partner on this. We ended up doing a pitch competition and got second place. The judges were very supportive and told us to reach out to them when we had a prototype.

Ethan: Yeah, I think another thing to add to that is in the beginning, we didn't really know what exactly it was going to be. We just had the idea of vitamins with honey and thought we'd see where that goes. I was a little tentative about the idea at first. I was thinking from a health perspective. Why would you mix vitamins with sugar? That defeats the whole purpose! But as we developed the idea and the messaging, it made more sense as an easier way to get your vitamins in a way that's different from pills and has fewer bad ingredients than typical gummy vitamins. So that's kind of what sold me.

James: I did another pitch competition while Ethan was studying abroad. I got third place. I took that money and bought a honey-spinning machine that was like a giant centrifuge. Ethan and I were ready to prototype and mix vitamin honey in our kitchen. For a little while, it kind of looked like a giant meth lab.

ENTREPRENEURIAL VOICES

Ethan: The honey spinning machine was great for prototyping, but at the end of the day, we couldn't sustain that. So, we were just trying to figure out who we can get to manufacture this really weird particular product, who has the certifications we need, is fine with handling vitamins, and has the capability of making these little honey sticks. There are only a handful of people in the country who meet these requirements.

James: As we started building this thing, we got approached by one of our friends who worked for an advertising agency. He wanted to work with us to change our branding and get us established. I was very attached to the name Vitamin Honey, and I liked the logo we just created. While consulting with our friend I had to separate myself from that attachment and my ego to progress our company to the next stage. We needed to get better branding, and get a more encompassing, friendlier name, and color scheme. So that was one of the first pivots I had to make personally for the betterment of the company. I had to detach myself from the solo idea to leave an opportunity for growth. Going forward, we started developing better packaging, and had our name changed from Vitamin Honey to Bizi.

Ethan: We assumed our marketing would just get sales right off the bat. We didn't really have a realistic understanding of the market and how much money it takes to advertise a product. We thought we had this new unique idea. We'll just use these preexisting already popular vitamins to sell them. But we found out that we're still competing with all the vitamin B, C, and D products with which the markets are completely saturated. It's super hard to do, even if you have a slightly new idea. And that's where we had to pivot most recently.

Keeping the same idea of vitamin-infused honey, we changed to the up-and-coming vitamins and supplements that are trending right now, that people are demanding and that the market has yet to meet that demand. We wanted to get in on the new supplements that are coming up to build a consumer base instead of trying to compete with all these other giant corporations producing D, C, and B who are spending millions in ads which we can't do.

James: Our new product is called Super Honey. It's got bee propolis, ginkgo, bee pollen, royal jelly, and ginseng. It's pretty tasty!

And now we're positioning our products more like a gummy vitamin. Gummy vitamins taste good, but they have a lot of extra additives in them.

Where we taste good, but there's no extra additives in our products. We've transitioned our strategy to look at our competitors and see what they're offering. That way we can see what is up and coming and provide a product that people really want.

Ethan: When doing something new and different, it's hard to educate consumers. Big companies have a lot of marketing dollars behind them, and they can afford to do a big campaign. We're trying to do it on a small scale, keep the ad budget low, and just do small growth, which I don't think is really working well for our product.

James: Same idea. New product. We don't necessarily steal market share away from the existing competitor but really build off it. And that's why our newest product we released is based on some trends we've observed and we added more elements to it to give it more value.

Ethan: The way we wanted to sell initially was through our website, which, again, you need to have a lot of advertising dollars to do that. The people in our price range aren't really making money unless they're already big. And those who aren't making money are trying to convert people to their website through Facebook and Google ads.

We looked into selling to grocery stores, but that didn't really work out because we didn't have any sales behind us to prove that we would be successful in a retail store. It's hard to get distributors on board. We were just doing small-dollar mom and pop shops, which weren't making us a ton of money, and we realized there was just so much work just to get one sale.

So, then we pivoted to doing Amazon. It was a hard decision because there's so many fees involved. You're subject to this other company. For instance, they could take down our product at any time just for some random violation, then we would have to talk to their computer chat system to fix it.

But, when you advertise on Amazon, you're advertising to the people who are already inclined to buy. They're already looking at stuff. It's basically like they're in a store. When you're advertising people on social media, people are just going about their day watching entertainment, consuming media, and then you interrupt them with some product sales pitch. Most of the time, they completely ignore it. Don't give it the time of day. That was a big factor as to why we weren't selling a ton and weren't really able to make the business profitable.

ENTREPRENEURIAL VOICES

Amazon is working well. We have a strategy in place. Right now, our price is reduced. We're just trying to get as much sales as we can so that we start ranking organically on certain keywords.

James: The whole time of going through these different strategies, we have been talking to other entrepreneurs, getting feedback from people. New ideas and fresh strategies from industry professionals are something we always appreciate.

Ethan: We always reach out to people and ask questions. Because when we started, we weren't experts in anything. So, we had to talk to the experts, get their opinion and integrate their information into our business. We talked to nutritionists, dietitians, then, more recently, marketing people to figure out the landscape.

James: Once we talked to them, we had to narrow down and absorb their information. We had to be able to discern what is good information for our company and what fit within our strategy.

Ethan: A lot of them contradict each other. One person might say one thing, and another person might contradict that. I think the hard part to is to figure out who's right, or if anyone's right. Then talk to even more people. It's like, thirty percent of people are saying this. Seventy percent of people are saying this. Also, does that person have a company we want to emulate? This guy helping us now came along, and his business is exactly where we want to be in five years. That's how we want it structured. We're thinking, yeah, that's something we want to emulate. So, we're going to listen.

James: From talking with other entrepreneurs in the industry we found someone we trusted. He launched a vitamin gummy company that's low in sugar. His brand had similar core values. I was nervous initially to reach out to him, especially because he's our direct competitor. Why would I want to talk to him? But then we reached out. He was actually a super friendly guy. He told us, "Yeah, I want to help you guys succeed. I'll tell you my pitfalls and what not to do because I blew $500,000 without even trying."

Ethan: He made the same mistake we did by trying to build up a website and get traction there. And he had a much larger failure than we ever did. So, he said, "Just stick with Amazon. I'll help you guys out. I know all this keyword stuff since I've done it before."

James: Yeah, it's been two years since we created the first prototype. Outside activity is a 100% necessity. I know that I'm a super social person, so just being able to talk and even just get support from friends and do other things outside is important. I have a side hustle of making music for a podcast in Dallas. I enjoy that because that's something I'm passionate about. It gives me a little way to do something else to take my mind off of Bizi . And also, therapy. Therapy is great. My therapist is also a business consultant. He's able to give great motivational insight when I feel stuck. It has reminded me to take a step back and look at how far we've come from day one. On day one, we had a piece of paper, and now we're at a full-blown real business that created something that didn't exist before.

Ethan: Yeah, I think at the end of the day, even if it fails, I still feel like I got a lot out of it, and there's a lot I learned. I mean, I have more knowledge about all these different areas of starting a business. If we restarted it, we could probably be where we are at half the time. So that seems reassuring. We made all the mistakes. We started the company right out of college. If I had a family right now, I don't think I would have the time to make these mistakes. I am hopeful that it will do well. But in the worst case, if it just goes down in flames, I still have a lot to take away from it.

James: Totally. It is really cool to know that this product literally didn't exist; we created it. I'm like, "Wow, we actually created something new!" That's so cool.

Chapter 26

Cassie Schreiner

I first got to know Cassie when she was a student of mine at Belmont. She had a clear vision that she would be a full-time wedding photographer and open a wedding venue when she graduated. I lost touch with Cassie after graduation. Years later, I caught up with her. She had a clear plan for her entrepreneurial career plan in college. Once she graduated, it took many interesting twists and turns!

I told myself I would never move back to Michigan. And here I am, back in Michigan.

I wanted to stay in Nashville. I felt like there was more money in Nashville. But it just wasn't clicking like it was in Michigan. It just seemed like I didn't have the people of Nashville behind me like I did in Michigan. I tried really hard to make connections in Nashville. I was constantly trying to find anyone to let me in so that I could get my wedding photography business rolling. But I just kept getting repeat referrals from Michigan. So, I moved back to Michigan to pursue wedding photography and build a wedding venue.

And that's why I ended up with this 15-acre farm where I was going to have a wedding venue. I did all my homework. I was a freshly graduated college student and thought I was doing everything right. I checked with township and county officials and convinced my parents that it was a no-brainer. Easy money.

There are a lot of different styles and offerings, but nobody in Michigan was doing it the way I was. I always say that trends in Michigan were probably 3 to 5 years behind Nashville. Learning photography in Nashville was great because I learned all the newest trends and where Michigan would soon be headed. Instead of the traditional formal photos they were getting in Michigan, I was different. I wasn't doing big-city Michigan weddings. I wasn't doing Detroit or Grand Rapids. I was in Frankenmuth, which is a smaller town known for its tourism.

I'm more of a photojournalist, so I like to capture the moment, as cheesy as it sounds. I don't want to make you feel stiff. I want you to be who you are. I want to capture a relationship. I want the loving moments. I want the funny ones. I want all of it. So, you get a good variety. I work my butt off, and I think people recognize that I'm going to be there for them. There are very, very few photographers that will do that. They might not remember what I said, but they will remember how I made them feel.

I bought the farm and started working on it right away, thinking the quicker we get it taken care of and fixed up, the quicker we can start making money. There were probably 400 trees that we cleared. We had two barns taken down because they were falling apart. We brought the Amish in to fix the main barn.

We were at the point where the township told me I needed to get their approvals and inspections done. I told them we were ready. And then they said, "Oh, well, you can't do that. You can't have a wedding venue."

It pretty much ruined my life for a while.

They said they thought it would be a bed and breakfast. Basically, what we found out is that my township is super corrupt. There are a lot of insider issues. The county officials are constantly in the news now about all the things they've done wrong. They've stolen money, laundered money, and the list goes on and on.

For the next year, they harassed me. They would sit at the end of my driveway. They would send me bills for cutting down dead trees. It just never ended. They even forged letters they said were from my neighbors. They told me I was a stupid girl who didn't know anything. It was awful.

I just stopped fighting them. I gave up and said, "That's it. I'm moving back to Tennessee. Forget it." My parents are like, "You just bought this farm. You're not moving."

So now our 15 acres has been groomed into the perfect location for photography sessions. Many of my clients enjoy coming to our home to have their photos taken. It is convenient to have a location available with so much variety and space.

It did become a little stressful always welcoming clients into our home. Frantically cleaning and making sure it was presentable for my sessions almost every day became a chore I didn't enjoy. It felt like our home couldn't be "lived in". It got to the point for three or four years where I was so booked that literally every single day I had a session. In 2020 I made the jump to raise my pricing. In fact, I nearly doubled every price I was offering. Raising prices is really hard if you don't get into the habit of it. I hadn't raised them in probably ten years, which is kind of embarrassing. But I was comfortable. I was happy with the people I was working with. I told myself they wouldn't spend more.

This was the beginning of huge growth for my business, which lead to having enough capital to build a separate studio on site. The studio is amazing. It has a bathroom for client use, as well as space for meetings and indoor photos. It has been a huge asset for the winter months. I have also been able to launch my boudoir side of my business with hopes of growing that to be a larger part of my income.

Last year, I told myself I was going to limit how many sessions I did a week. But I didn't do that. I just have this looming doomsday-prepping husband who keeps talking about a recession. So, I'm like, "Eventually, people are going to stop paying me these higher prices, so I just better take it while I can."

***

I thrive from the pressure of weddings. I'm kind of a control freak. I come into somebody's life who's planning the most important day and doesn't really know much because they've never done this before. I guide them and tell them what to do and what not to do. I coordinate and run the timeline and make sure everybody's doing what they're supposed to be doing behind the scenes. A lot of photographers just show up and do their job. I'm in rural Michigan. Wedding planners aren't really a thing like they are in a big city with $100,000 budget weddings. I help plan and then make sure the wedding day runs smoothly.

My big ones are Christmas "minis." My setups are huge. I bought a Jeep panel wagon to stack presents on top of. I have covered my entire barn wall with Christmas signs, kind of like Cracker Barrel. COVID was the year that it really took off. I think I had 60 families come in over two or three days. And they're quick. They're 15 minutes, and I do them back-to-back. I don't leave any wiggle room. We orchestrate it all, and it's fast. In two days, I make anywhere between $10,000 and $30,000. My husband helps. My mom comes. I tell them every year that I'm just going to hire someone to do their jobs, but they kind of get offended. I also do fall minis, but they're not quite as big. And now that I have a studio built, I'm going to pick back up Easter minis, where I rent a baby lamb from a farm for kids to be with.

The Christmas minis are pretty big. It's the last hurrah of the year. And then I die!

Around the end of 2020, I was burnt out. There was a moment where I was like, "I quit. I don't want to do this anymore. I hate this. I am so tired. Is this the only thing I do with my life? You know, we don't have friends." I was at the point where I would just like to go and be a train conductor somewhere. It sounds lovely, doesn't it?

It's hard to have friends because you can't do anything when normal people do things on the weekends. I was just at a breaking point. Andy is a wedding deejay. He runs a branch of the credit union during the week. Andy's a loan officer and kills it at that. And then, on the weekends, he does deejaying. I probably make him do way too much for me. He's my furniture mover. He's moving furniture all over the farm for photos. I have projects for him all the time. He kind of wants to quit deejaying. He's transitioning to only doing weddings with me.

***

I would really like to get a herd of alpacas. And sell socks. That's what I want to do. I want to have baby alpacas. Right now, I don't feel like I'm present enough to have baby animals. Birth is a big deal. I'm not going to be having any children, so I would like baby alpacas. Yeah.

We've been visiting alpaca farms everywhere we go. No matter where we are, I always look for an alpaca farm. There's one in Ohio, and their model is so different. They make more money off people just coming to pet the alpacas than they do off actually selling socks.

I figure if I ever quit to be an alpaca farmer, the studio we built can become my alpaca boutique. Or it can be an Airbnb and continue to make revenue.

Chapter 27

Asher Segelken

Asher Segelken grew up in Southern California as an active church member. Asher took his passion for his faith and found a higher purpose in his business, Good Grain Creative, LLC.

Good Grain was originally going to be a film festival, but I had the idea of combining many different things, and it was this big, messy idea. I was having coffee with a mentor of mine, C.J. Cassiotta, over at the factory in Franklin. He stops me in the middle of my little dream fest, just laying out this idea to him, and I go into a metaphor about how whatever this thing becomes, it'll deliver Good Grain, cultivating the best of (films at the time) and sending them into the world. He stops me in the middle of that and says, "Whatever you do with this, that's what it's called, you have to call it Good Grain, there's something there."

I grew up in Orange County, California. The churches that were founded there are the pioneers of the mega-church movement. Right now, some micro-church movements pioneered in America are also coming out of California as a response to megachurches. I've always loved ministry. I've always had a toe in it, whether leading worship or just doing ministry videos. God's always been in it with me somehow. It's always been fulfilling work coming alongside scrappy, entrepreneurial people who want to make a good impact in the world. I've just been soaked in spiritual entrepreneurship my whole life. Looking back on it now, it was stupid for me to think I wouldn't end up somewhere with ministry in some capacity, whether it was a mindset or, in this case, a whole business.

However, I didn't always want to be an entrepreneur. I wanted to be the next Steven Spielberg like any other kid in Southern California with a video camera. Before doing marketing for ministries, I was in video, mentored by Award-winning filmmaker Brandon Setter of Setter Studios. My approach to business and to marketing would be lightyears behind where it is if it were not for Brandon's friendship, generosity, and mentorship to me over the years, teaching me how to use a camera, hear a story, tell a story, and establish a business that prioritizes relationships and service. I still remember it like it was yesterday. Brandon and I were at a Starbucks around the corner from the church, and he sat me down and said "Asher, don't make the same mistake I did by getting a film degree. Get an entrepreneurship degree. It's much more versatile. Plus, I see you as someone who might hire me to tell his story or stories in the future." Little did I know how prophetic that moment would be! Thank God for Brandon Setter.

Later, as a Junior in college in 2019, I was doing customer discovery research. I laid out three options: nonprofits, churches, and art. And so, I started looking into where I thought I could fit in and fill a need. I blamed God and the algorithm for what happened next, but I "stumbled on" five articles about how the church was losing millennials and how it was a huge question. And I remember thinking, "Why is Church so hard to communicate?" At that point, reluctantly, I knew that ministries were where Good Grain would end up.

I started doubling down on the idea of churches. I interviewed 50 or 60 pastors. Some were from metro areas as big as Philadelphia and Los Angeles. One of the interviews was with a pastor I grew up with out in California named Josh Harrison. During his interview, my heart broke for him and smaller churches. I thought, "I want to try and find a workflow and a pricing structure for *this* type of church, not necessarily a megachurch, but a smaller/newer church."

During my research, I learned that megachurches are looking for congregant relationship management systems that can track every interaction that every person has with their gospel presentation. And the more data points you could provide in a system like that, the better. But for smaller churches, what they need is a little bit more simple, more fundamental. They need somebody who can do a website, email, and social media for under $10,000 a year. So, I went to the drawing board and started looking at reliable and simple strategies I could implement for thousands of churches for a reasonable price. After a bit of work, God let me find strategies and workflows that could accommodate that initial price point. Shoutout to Pastor Joshua Harrison for laying out this value proposition so perfectly.

The hardest part, initially, was stepping away from video production and photography because I had done that for about eight or nine years. I thought for a long time that's how I would make my money and my name in the world. It was a sobering moment. Yet what has been my life's work since, has been much more fulfilling than I could have ever dreamed of when I was younger. If it were not for Jeff Cornwall confronting me with this necessary step along with many others during the research process at Belmont, Good Grain would not have become the focused business it is today. Like many others, I am so thankful for his wisdom and generosity, which has been the difference between businesses being dreams and realities.

I usually pick up with churches at two parts of their story, either at the beginning or well along the way. I work with established churches over one hundred years old or church planters who are just as entrepreneurial as I am and have launched recently or are about to launch. My clients and I connect on that adventurous, entrepreneurial level, and then I manage their digital communications. There's a church I work with that says that every single time we post something on social media, they get five new people in a week. My job is to get people to the church for the first time. Becoming a member is more of the selling process by the pastor that happens once they enter the church doors.

I was working with a church I loved that was set to renew my biggest contract. Their executive pastor, who was my point person, left. About 24 hours later, I was notified that my contract would be terminated once completed. About half of my income came from that one client. It was a little bit of a nightmare. Something I learned from it is that it's not official until it's official. It's not them saying, "Oh, we're planning on this, it's when the credit card gets charged that it's real." When that church dropped, that day was my worst day because the company was still so young. There was a moment when I thought it would not make it to its 3rd year. I only had seven clients, and this was my one large one. I said, "God, you got to come through. You're the boss." I would be the first to admit God is very confusing. You sometimes lose the sense of optimism and security, but if you hold on long enough, he'll come through.

As of this writing, we've touched 20 or 25 different ministries, both churches and para-church ministries. The initial offerings include a website, email, and social media. We get them up and running and provide channel management regularly. We don't create any content as an agency, which is unique because most agencies do *all* the content. I talked with Southern Californian Christian entrepreneur Keith Page. He is the founder of the church that I grew up in. He said, "You might be lucky to edit some videos. You're not going to be making them. You need the churches to find the volunteers who will give their time and resources to either shoot the photo or shoot the video and then send it to you to post." We help plan the campaigns and then give them to the churches to develop the content assets. We then take the content from them, put it through the channels, and market it.

We've recently added graphic design services that have gotten many great responses, including sermon series branding, event branding, logos, and easy stuff like that. It's just fundamental graphics, kind of cut and paste. I'm also thinking about possibly adding a lot more à la carte services, including video and photo editing, graphics, website design, campaign design, and things like that. It'd be fun as the business grows to get back into doing some media projects again.

***

Time and time again, there is an incredible tension between my identity as a ministry leader and a business owner. How does one navigate the situation where he or she is a stakeholder in some respect to every party in the deal? I run Good Grain Creative, but I am a Christian, and I want these ministries to succeed no matter what. In the moments when ministries mistreat me, and it happens more often than I care to admit, I have to remember that ministries are run by people and that in the moments when I take the high road to avoid conflict to maintain the peace between believers, that those actions are not happening in secret or in the dark, that God will right my generosity from duress in the longer run. This difference defines a ministry from a business, how we treat long-run decisions in the short run. Here's a quick example a client decided not to pay for a three-year contract they agreed to. As much as I wanted to get what I was owed, I decided to mark the contract as uncollectable and to move on from the situation because I knew by doing that, God would care for me later on. Faith allows for mercy, allows for grace, allows for space, allows for a broader paradigm to be in the driver's seat regarding financial security and entrepreneurial viability. It's trusting that in the end God put you on the path and he'll get you to the destination. The best thing to do in the meantime is to follow God because he's worthy of our trust, and worthy to be followed and obeyed. I'm still in business because God sees fit to keep me in business, serving churches by helping them tell their stories and, for that, I will always be grateful.

Chapter 28

Clark Buckner

Clark Buckner has had an entrepreneurial spirit since he was a young child. In grade school, he found ways to turn classmates into customers. He made "fun packs" of handmade mazes, sold Pokémon cards, and became a wholesaler of hacky sacks. His creativity led him into marketing, which eventually led him to podcasting. Relationary Marketing, the company Clark co-founded, is an agency that produces branded podcasts for B2B content marketing.

I started listening to podcasts in 2011 or 2012. I started to see its power. I realized that podcasting was really just a different form of media.

I had started a little business doing branding, making WordPress websites, and other basic marketing stuff. Podcasting became a part of that. Podcasting can be a good tool in marketing. My business partner Chuck and I knew each other by volunteering in Nashville's marketing meet-up community. It was a really vibrant meet-up community. Back then, I was really hard on myself, really anxious. You hear a lot of success is driven by anxiety which has fueled me. I'm trying to channel it in a productive way, but I'm also trying to untangle some of that stuff now. In that marketing meet-up community, I found a lot of belonging.

I tried to get an entry point at the EC[19] because I saw that they needed help with social media. I also pitched the idea of them doing a podcast. I also had to convince my wife, Hope, because, at this point, we were newly married. She loves stability. Being an entrepreneur does not always create stability. But she trusted me and supported my dreams to launch my own efforts. That's about the time when I started Relationary Marketing with my business partner Chuck. We started hiring independent contractors to help with the podcast editing work, and from there we built an agency together. It was good timing.

It's been a good business relationship for us. It is like a marriage. It is 50/50. It's just always worked. We are very different and balance each other. He is 55, and I'm 31. He likes to travel the world. He's doing the digital nomad thing, spending a lot of time in Asia. Sometimes it's hard with the 12-hour time difference, but we find a way, even in times of

---

[19] Nashville Entrepreneur Center

challenge . At this point, we're both pretty much full-time doing Relationary Marketing.

He has been a great business partner. It's been a good balance. For example, he helps lead our contracts and other on-going tasks like payroll. He's good at that. I fill in more as the face of the company and help lead the creative side.

I've always had this interest in working with students and being a resource to them. And so, I've had probably 60 or 70 interns over the course of 7 years. A lot of our talent at our company is homegrown that way. Sometimes they stick with us. Sometimes they want to go get a full-time job. But either way, they are a part of our little crew. That's been a big part of our growth. Chuck has a similar passion for mentorship. He's taught me a lot.

During COVID, we were able to stay open. A lot of our contractors are musicians. During COVID, they could not tour anymore. They said, "Hey, we need more work." We dialed up their work so they could do more with us until the music business picked up again.

***

Traditional podcasts have more of a B2C strategy. They've got a big podcast, they sell ads, that's how they create value. We don't do that. We have a B2B strategy. We help clients build credibility with their customers and help promote big events. Our podcasts help them deliver engaging content for their content marketing plan. I often say podcasts don't make money, but content marketing makes money. Podcasting can make for great content marketing. Podcasting is a tool. How are you using your content to drive change? If it's an internal podcast, like what we do at Bridgestone, there are ways to show success. They have 50,000 employees. They need to have an internal communication strategy. The podcast gives their CEO a chance to talk a lot about their "North Star." I'll tell my clients that it's all about the podcast working for you, not you working for the podcast. It is just another communication and marketing tool.

The Nashville Software School has been interviewing all their graduates in their podcasts. It's a five-to-ten-minute interview to briefly give their story. They'll share what they've built for their demo day capstone. And then, they talk about what they want to do next. I've interviewed 2000 graduates. It's a helpful tool for a couple of reasons. Employers can't meet every student who had a graduation demo day, but they can listen to the podcast and hear that high-level overview. Also, often while I'm interviewing an NSS graduate, they mention how listening to the podcast helped them see themselves and understand how they might be able to be successful as NSS.

When someone thinks of my name, I want them to think about podcasting. If you search Nashville podcasting or Nashville podcaster, you'll usually find me on that first page.

JEFFREY CORNWALL

SECTION 5

IN SEARCH OF BALANCE

"Never get so busy making a living that you forget to make a life."
Dolly Parton

Chapter 29

Jen, Susan, and Jadon

My wife and I had returned to our hometown of Ripon, Wisconsin, for a high school class reunion (we were high school sweethearts). At the venue where we had our gathering, J's BBQ, I started talking with Jen, who, along with Susan, are the owners. She shared a lot about their entrepreneurial journey. Luckily, I had my interview recording kit along. I asked if I could sit with them and discuss their story. They are very private people but agreed to meet with me.

I sat in the kitchen of their home just outside of Ripon with Jen, Susan, and their son Jadon.

From their website: "Jadon suffered a stroke at birth and later developed Cerebral Palsy and a grand mal seizure disorder. He was a fighter and a survivor since birth. I [Susan] had envisioned naming the BBQ joint of my dreams...after Jadon, because as a family, we would do whatever it takes to make J's BBQ nothing less than AMAZING in honor of him! It would be our lifeline, our present, our future with and for Jadon."

Jen: I was the General Manager in Ripon at a bowling alley. Connected to the building, there was a space that a restaurant was moving out of.

I asked Susan, "Do you want to open a restaurant?" Her eyes lit up and she said, "Yes! It's got to be barbecue though!" I was like, "No, it's got to be a supper club."

Susan: An opportunity like that doesn't just surface randomly in one's lifetime.

Why barbecue?

Susan: I grew up in Texas, and developed a love for barbeque. People seek out good barbecue, because it's welcoming to all, inviting and delicious!

Jen: Growing up in the Northwoods, we grilled brats, burgers and steaks. Perfecting Prime Rib and a Friday night fish fry was every Wisconsin Supper Clubs specialty. However, the process of smoking was completely foreign to me. As for brisket… what's that?

ENTREPRENEURIAL VOICES

Susan: It was the ultimate dream for us both, owning a restaurant that would allow me the flexibility for and with Jadon. I could drop all other hat(s), while having security and comfort that my partner in life and in business would hold the restaurant down (for us) no matter what. We were a devoted family; from the get go, and our mutual love and respect for this delicate balance was natural.

We approached Mike Vaughan at Fortifi Bank for a small loan. We probably looked nothing short of crazy, respectfully speaking. Two women and a special needs young boy contacting a local bank (not natives to the area), saying we want to start a restaurant. We have ample experience in addition to the necessary education backgrounds, and we've got the passion. Well, after further discussion and seeing our business plan, Mike had faith in *us* and said, "Okay, we'll give you a good Samaritan loan of $30,000."

Most would agree that $30,000, in the bigger picture, is not a lot of money to start out. Preparing a venue, purchasing kitchen equipment (including a smoker that neither of us knew how to work), inventory and creating an ambiance that says "barbecue." The old banquet carpet and layers upon layers of carpet glue and screaming colors had to be dealt with, and were no easy task. Thankfully, I have a love for design, so my $1000 budget was enough for some rustic pieces and a LOT of paint.

Jen: After, I'd say a couple of months, we started to establish a bit of a line. Friday nights and other peak hours, it eventually got to the point where our line would extend outside into the parking lot, and people were waiting to get in! I remember Susan and I would look at each other and feel like, oh, my gosh, this is happening.

You're from Texas. You're from the Northwoods. You come to Ripon, bringing in this new concept as outsiders. How did you deal with that?

Susan: Of the few handfuls of people that knew us, they were supportive. I think they were nervous for us, given our diverse family, and the fact that we chose a male-dominated venture with BBQ. I think others had a good laugh, if not a few choice words behind our backs. The truth is…when you're outsiders, no one knows what you're capable of. We believe that's a huge part of the entrepreneurial spirit that feeds the fire.

How did you win this little town over?

Susan: Be who you are, and share it boldly and confidently as professionals. Jen and I created J's BBQ from the passion in our hearts and our love for the industry… experience that extends beyond 50 years. If you open your doors to provide a service and an experience, you have to remain focused on your business, its purpose and goals. We never opened our restaurant with the mindset of being the best in BBQ or the best restaurant in town, but rather to do what we committed to, doing the best we can. It's about being a community team player, supporting others while steadying a path toward your own success.

How did you transition to your own space on Main Street?

Jen: We were two weeks away from hanging it up, actually. Being done. We were ready to leave that space. We outgrew that kitchen's capacity within a year, and it became near impossible to meet the demands. We searched and searched a 50-mile radius for a venue that could support our growth, and nothing was adding up.

It felt like one of those defining moments for us. How can we realistically keep doing this?

Our circumstances became known around town, and we started to get approached.

Susan: The college was the biggest motivating factor. Students were walking from campus to the bowling alley (1.7 miles) for J's BBQ. Zach Messitte [president of Ripon College] had a private meeting with us in his office and said, "You two are fabulous. You two are mentors to so many of our students. We need to find a way to bridge the gap between campus and downtown. We need J's BBQ downtown for so many reasons."

Jen: We had been serving a bigger purpose than we even realized. We brought diversity and inclusion to the community and we are excelling beyond our wildest dreams…we couldn't stop! We essentially made a pact with the college. We would utilize the restaurant side, and the college would utilize the bar side for their mercantile and study shop.

Susan: In late 2018, the college came to us and said that the space wasn't working for them as they'd hoped it would. So, we assumed their contract and turned it into a whiskey-bourbon bar called "The Other Side" offering table service and dining for patrons 21+. IT took off!

ENTREPRENEURIAL VOICES

Jen: Then COVID hit.

We created an online ordering system for curbside pick-up within 48 hours of the shutdown. It showed our heartbeat. It showed passion and drive. The tone was saying we're coming together. We had regular customers driving from Milwaukee for takeout just to bring back to Milwaukee, because everything was shut down. Several Chicago patrons made the trip just to order 10+ pounds of brisket and catering trays of mac and cheese! Once we started to see that, we began shipping to four states in the Midwest and created an in-house "Country Store" offering vacuum sealed meats, sauces, homestyle sides, apparel & more!

We made it. We made it debt free. Our backgrounds, our passion, our drive... we are always making decisions for the right reason. Our strength only continued to prevail through what we were able to do; not only as a family, but as a couple, as a partnership. Nothing has been easy, but we definitely have shown that we will always persevere. We are as devoted to our brand as we are our family, and that's priceless.

How do you sustain this to keep it going?

Susan: Well, funny you ask because we're at the beginning of our exit plan with the restaurant, as franchising was never a desired option. We've always known this part (the brick and mortar) of our brand is not something we planned on doing long-term. We want a better balance for our family, while the brand continues to grow. Reconfiguring our balance is where we're at right now.

Our demand has once again exceeded our kitchen's capacity, and our family's needs continue to persist. In order to put our next plan into place, we need to shift gears. If you become stagnant or trapped as an entrepreneur, if your current business plan reaches a plateau...you've lost the momentum and everyone feels it.

Sacrifice, risk and progression.... it's all part of the journey. We are humble and proud. From a $30,000 start to a multi-million dollar mini-empire brand: J's BBQ. We created, built and operated this business single-handedly with zero investors, while mastering the MOST AMAZING brisket, and creamiest mac and cheese, EVER!

A customer once said to us, "Take this to heart in the best way possible. J's BBQ could never be duplicated. Somebody else could never run 'J's BBQ' the way that you, Jen, and Jadon do J's BBQ. That's the mystique and magic of experiencing J's BBQ."

Jen: We reminisce about the first pound of pulled pork we sold. We looked at each other with eyes wide open, like, oh my God, we don't even have a container for it! What are we going to put this in?! Barbeque *is* more than just a sandwich and two sides. People were starting to request meats by-the-pound!! It was in that moment that we started creating the catering business, because we both knew it was only a matter of time.

Susan: It's a blessing, but also a curse that it happened so early on... catering took off overnight, and with proper licensing, certifications and a BPA (blanket purchase agreement) for the Federal Government, J's BBQ is honored to cater ten Wisconsin National Guards, in addition to over a thousand statewide private, business and corporate events every year. It's outlandishly insane how much food goes out of our kitchen, and needless to attempt to explain the efforts behind *that* volume of production.

[Susan says to Jen] Just for shits and giggles, tell him how many pounds of meat just went out. She'll do this every now and then because we'll look at each other and we can't even fathom how much product just went out the back of the house... but it happens all the time.

Jen: We're only open four days a week, so last week it was about 400 pounds of pork and close to 1,200 pounds of brisket. That's just two of our meats.

Have you let yourselves dream about what might be next?

J's BBQ brand is still very much alive. We are in the early stages of wholesale and production. Perhaps it too will once again exceed our wildest dreams... time tells all.

Susan: As for our family...we're explorers, and we love adventure. One of the best forms of education for Jadon, is exposure to diversity and culture. We just want to be able to do more with him, as a family.

It's easy to get lost or caught up in success, and perhaps forget about or even disregard the need for an exit strategy. It's dangerous to become oblivious to the cycle. If you begin to lose yourself, stop and evaluate if the exit is nearing. It could be 5 years; it could be 30 years. No matter how long you commit to a business, we believe exit strategies should be included in every business plan. Afterall, we've only got one chance at this short thing called "life." In all that we do and all that we are…we're 100% committed to doing and being the best, we can.

Jen: As I always say, every business had to start somewhere, it's about teachable moments, growing, and always moving forward.

Chapter 30

Meredith Mazie

Like so many other people, Meredith Mazie moved to Nashville to become a country music star.

And it turned out that I didn't like being in the spotlight. On the Enneagram, I'm a nine, which is the peacemaker. I don't like confrontation. I like being in my own little space. I don't like being the center of attention. And once I took that test, even I was like, "Oh, this all makes sense. It's all coming together now."

I started dressing everybody while I was working retail. And all of my friends were like, "Hey, can we go shopping? I love your style. I made commercial showcase. Can we go shopping for that?"

This was fun. It combined my love for music and fashion, but I was behind the scenes, which is where I like to be, instead of being that performer on stage in front of everybody. I realized this other path could still be a way of having a creative outlet. It just didn't look like what I thought it would or what growing up I imagined my life would be, which is not a bad thing. We're supposed to grow and change as we get older and go through different experiences. I think it was the time for me to really realize that.

Once I graduated, I still did the same thing with styling people working for a booking agency. My boss at the time asked me if I could take his daughter shopping for her Christmas present. There wasn't really a place to go for what she was looking for that was what I wanted to provide outside of fast fashion, which is going to fall apart in two seconds.

I thought to myself, "There is something missing here in Nashville. Why can't I do that? And what does that look like? And how do I even start doing that?"

So, I started doing research. How do I open a business? How much money do I need? Am I an LLC? Luckily my dad owns his own business back in Virginia, so he was my sounding board. I called him probably too many times a day.

I was driving down 8th Avenue, and I had this epiphany. I said, "If now is not the time, then when will be the time? So, let's just take the plunge. If I fail, I fail. But what if I succeed?"

I feel that a lot of people don't think about what could go right. They really focus on the fear and what could go wrong. I feel like fear is the biggest thing that will hold us back in life. So, I would rather try something and fail than never even give it a shot. Let's just do it!

I got my business plan together. A lot of people start online, and then they move into the brick and mortar. But for me, I wanted to be present. I feel like you can't have that sort of customer relationship with a computer screen or a business that's solely online. Because I really wanted to be a part of the day-to-day experience and really be the face of the brand. So, I skipped online and went straight into brick-and-mortar. I didn't open my online store until six to nine months after I was open. Online is like a whole other business.

I had an appointment in Germantown. I drove by and saw the sign in the window of this building. It was the last space available. I thought I needed to call this person because I felt drawn to this place. It was scary because the neighborhood was not developed. Am I going into something that's not going to be walkable? I want to be in a high-traffic, locally driven area. So, I called the property manager, did a tour of the space, fell in love with it, and fell in love with the people here.

I signed the lease. I started off with 650 square feet. I carried men's and women's fashion because, at the time, I wanted to be inclusive and have something for everybody. But then I quickly realized that men just don't shop as much as we do. I invested all this time, money, and energy, going on buying trips going to L.A. and finding all these brands for them to just sit in the store. So, I had to pivot, which I feel is all you do in business. Opening the shop was probably the hardest thing I've ever done, but looking back, I wouldn't change any of it. And that's where the name of the store, Abednego, comes from. It's from my favorite story in the Bible. The three of them are in the fiery furnace. Because of their faith, they came out alive. And you know, everyone goes through fires in life. I've gone through my fair share of trials, and I've chosen to come out on the other side. I embrace what these trials have done for me and the growth I've been through to get to where I am today.

At the end of December 2019, I contacted my property manager because I was ready to expand. I told her, "I don't want to leave you guys. I love this complex, and I love the neighborhood. So, if any of the bigger spaces open up, please let me know."

She said, "Absolutely. It's so funny you said that because the business in the end space is actually leaving at the end of the year."

And I said, "Whoa, okay, well, that's like less than a month, but I'm here for it. Let's make it happen".

And now I need bigger "things." I need a bigger desk, a bigger fitting room, and double the inventory. I dump in probably $25,000, maybe $30,000 into this new space for Abednego.

I reopened in February 2020. I'm open for maybe three weeks, and then the tornado comes through. I hear that it's ripped through Germantown. I called my friends who live down the street. I said, "Can you please just go walk up the street and rip the Band-Aid off for me? Like, is it there, or is it gone?"

And they walked up and said, "Meredith, there is literally not a hanger out of place."

I was crying hysterically. It came down Jefferson. It hit everything here, and then it just picked up and missed our whole building. I thought, "I don't understand. There are people in the Jefferson apartment complex who were pulled out of their windows, and here I am, nothing out of place."

We ended up popping up at L+L Market on Charlotte in their just big open warehouse space. And we were there until our power got turned back on, which was wonderful. The power was turned back on for a week, and then we got the news that COVID was happening. We soon got the "stay at home order." But I have placed orders 6 to 8 months in advance. So, I'm still getting shipments in. I would have to come into the store, even though I'm not making any money. I'm just spending money as inventory is coming in. Luckily, our property managers and landlords were amazing. They helped us with rent.

I was pivoting again. How do I use social media to my advantage? How do I still get the products out there? I could still buy the inventory I knew people wanted, which now was sweatpants, matching pajama sets, slippers, socks, and gift cards. I was running a special on those. I felt like drinking, eating, and online shopping were the only things you could do.

I remember my husband and I would go for a walk, and we'd say, "Do you want an Aperol spritz on the way? It's 10 a.m. Why not!" We started this thing that we still do today. It's called Clothes and Cocktails. During COVID, whenever I would get a new shipment, I would get on social media and do stories. I would do live trials of all the new stuff we had coming in. And then my husband would make a cocktail of the week. "This is what we're drinking this week. How about you? Look at these new clothes that you can still buy because, like, hey, we're still getting inventory, and we still want to be here." We still do it every Wednesday. I do try-ons, my husband makes the cocktail of the week, and we post it online. That's what got me through COVID. It was community support, people buying gift cards, and customers just wanting small businesses to still be here. It was a really humbling and emotional but a beautiful space to be in. As hard as it was, it showed people's true colors and was really nice to see. So that was probably my biggest fire!

I really feel like boutiques are the ones that are going to still survive all of this because you have that one-on-one interaction and a closely curated selection of items. I know everything about how it fits. I'm trying everything on. I've talked to the reps about it. You don't get that when you walk into Dillard's or shop online. I still get most of my sales from brick-and-mortar. Maybe about ten percent are from online sales.

How has your job changed from when you first opened up to today?

It's changed a lot. You know, within the past year, my husband and I were trying to start a family, which is scary. But then you have to think about your first baby, which is my store. Within the past year, I've really started to take a step back from day-to-day operations because I'm trying to prepare myself for what that might look like when I have a baby or, down the road, when my kid has an activity.

In the beginning, it was just me. I was closed on Mondays. That was my one day off to do errands and all that stuff. I didn't start paying myself until year three. And then I finally got to a point where I was like, I need a life. I need to not work every weekend. I was missing out on a lot of things, which is fine. You have to sacrifice when you're first starting something, which I was willing to do. But it gets to that point where like, I'm tired, I'm burnt out.

And that was affecting my business. I remember people would walk by, and I would say, "Please don't come in. Oh, my gosh, please don't come in. I'm so tired." That's not what you want for your business. I knew at that point that I needed help. I couldn't do this alone anymore. So, I got a weekend girl. And that was a game changer just to have every other weekend off to regroup.

I fell back in love with what I was doing. I don't ever want to think of this place as a burden. I want to really find joy in it. She was able to help me get back to that place, which was really nice. I had her for three years, and then we hired on a social media person because that alone is a full-time job that I didn't have time to do.

I can only do so much. And so bringing in different perspectives, different opinions, and views from all these new creative people has helped us grow. It's been a cool collaboration to see how it's shaped the business and grown into something more than I thought it would be. I'm one person. But when you bring in that community of creatives, it has an opportunity to grow into something much bigger, much cooler than I ever thought it could. So that's kind of where we are now. I have a manager that we just hired a year ago. She's like my right-hand gal.

It's really cool to be able to give people jobs that they value and appreciate and have fun with. I'll take that. Yes, please. I am doing this for myself and for Nashville. I'm doing it for our community. I'm doing it for the people who work for me. I'm doing it for people who come in and want to feel good about themselves and what they're wearing and have a positive experience and having an affordable place to do that. It's the people that come in and say, "Oh, my gosh, I wore this dress to my sister's wedding, and I got so many compliments on it. I felt so good about myself." I'm like, "Heck yes, girl."

In college, body image was such an important thing to me. It was an obsessive thing. And to see past that, see who you are, and feel comfortable with yourself, with how you are, is such an amazing thing. If I can help translate that through clothes to somebody, then that's worth it. That's success. Without sales, we wouldn't be here. But the best part is having those repeat customers come back in, knowing how good they feel, and knowing that we can provide that for them.

Chapter 31

Matt Fiedler

Matt Fiedler had a passion for music and a passion for business. Eventually, this led him to co-found Vinyl Me Please (VMP), a record-of-the-month club that offers exclusive vinyl record presses for its customers.

For the first year and a half, it was nights and weekends. I didn't make any money from it. It was just a passion project. My day job was just a day job, and I used the money I earned there to pay for my livelihood. But I came to life when I came home, and I was able to work on VMP. In those early days, it was very manual. We'd spend our nights packing records. We hand-wrapped each record, wrote handwritten thank you notes, and even hand-wrote addresses on each box. Then on the weekends, we'd have to borrow a car or walk them down to the post office.

We also spent a lot of time on the phone with our members. We'd try to connect with them, hear what they're listening to, and we'd share digital playlists with them.

It was incredibly time-consuming. Almost nothing was scalable in those early days.

How did you get from packing boxes on the weekends to quitting your day jobs and building a company?

It all came down to trust.

Early on, our singular focus was on ensuring our existing members had a positive experience. That's why we went to such great lengths to make everything as special as we could, despite so much of it being manual and unscalable. We earned trust by going above and beyond, and in return, our early members were patient with us as we worked out kinks in our systems and would stick around, even if they got a record they wouldn't like. They could sense our authenticity and our passion for what we were doing. They felt like they were a part of something bigger than themselves.

We also relied heavily on the trust and credibility the artists we were working with had with their audiences. We did everything we could to borrow their brand equity to bring credibility to VMP. So anytime we work with the new artist, we're like, "Can you post it on Twitter? Can you post it on Facebook? Can you send an email to your email list?" This was critical in helping recruit new members to the service.

And over time, as we continued to prove ourselves, more momentum was put into the flywheel. By 2014 – our second year -- potential members had several touchpoints through which they could reference and assess VMP. They could look at our archive, get a feel for our curation, and were likely to discover something new; they would see their friends posting about VMP on social media; they'd see the artist community engaged; major blogs started to talk about us; see us engaged in the broader community. All of that not only increased visibility of the brand but also contributed to a sense of excitement and validation. It became a lot easier for a potential member to join as a result.

By the end of year 1, we had about 300 members. By the middle of year two, we had about 1,500. By the end of year two, we had more than 5,500.

It was in the middle part of year two that we decided to go full-time on VMP. It was just too big to ignore at that point, and we knew we had an opportunity that wasn't going to last forever. It was a leap of faith and a signal that it was time to trust ourselves and in what we'd built to that point. We had no idea what VMP would eventually become, but we simply couldn't ignore what was happening.

After about two and a half years, we hit 10,000 members. It was so friggin' hard to get there, and it felt like such a meaningful mark.

At that point, there were still four or maybe five of us working on it. It was lunch tables in the basement, whiteboards, and shit all over the place. We had rented a house in suburban Denver that we were running our operations out of. We had semis pull up and just unload pallets of records, USPS trucks making multiple trips to pick up and ship the records. People coming and going all of the time. The neighbors had to think it was a drug den we were running there!

When we hit 10k, we didn't win an award, and nobody knocked on the door and said, "Congratulations! You've made it!" and still, we were so proud of ourselves. We popped champagne.

One thing I've learned is that whether it's going exceedingly well or incredibly poorly, it will soon pass. Shortly after we hit 10k members, we experienced one of the toughest seasons I can remember.

We were growing so quickly that it was hard to keep up with the inventory demands. We were bootstrapped at that point, and a large portion of our cash flow was used to fund inventory purchases. What's more, the manufacturing process was wildly complex. We leaned on our partners to handle manufacturing. This became an issue as we had several instances where our partners didn't care as much about our timelines as we did, and we had several instances where inventory was significantly delayed. This caused large disruptions in the business.

Our solution to this problem was to plan further and further out. We felt pretty good about our approach at the time. We forecasted what we thought was modest growth, made inventory commitments, and put cash down as an insurance policy against potential future delays.

Our forecasts ended up being off by a pretty wide margin. It's not that we stopped growing, we still grew at an impressive rate, but nothing close to what we forecasted. The gaps between the number of members we had each month and the amount of inventory we purchased got bigger each month. One month we committed to 15,000 records, but we only had 12,000 subscribers. The next month we had 14,000 subscribers with 18,000 records on order. And then, 15,000 subscribers and 20,000 records ordered. It was like compounding interest, but in a bad way.

The latter half of 2015 was probably the worst six months of my life. It was like a car wreck that was happening in slow motion. We could see the gap getting wider, but there wasn't much we could do about it in the short term. It was six months before we could make a change because all of our orders were locked in. Every day I felt like I was walking into the guillotine. I remember just being so ashamed of myself. I thought, "If we go out of business because we bought too many records, that is the dumbest reason possible for us to go out of business."

It ended up being a profound lesson, both in business and in leadership. We had moved from the house we rented to a proper office in Boulder. We had a few other full-time team members. There was a lot to be excited about; I could not bring myself to even smile. I was a total mope. I thought it was a foregone conclusion. We'd run out of money, lay off our team, and shut down. I couldn't imagine any other reality, and I carried those emotions into the office every day.

The leadership lesson comes from something one of my partners said. He pulled me aside one day and said, "Hey, man, I understand things are bad, but you have to recognize how you are showing up and how that's affecting the rest of the team. And even if you don't say anything, they're all picking up on what you're putting out. People are nervous, and everybody's scared to do anything because they don't know if they should be looking for another job or if this will all be fine. Your job as a leader is to help them understand the reality while still leading them. You need to change the way that you're showing up for the sake of everybody."

That was one of those conversations that changed the course of my life in a meaningful way. It was a hard lesson to learn, and we managed to get through it. I don't remember exactly what we did, but I know we had to get creative. We called a lot of our vendors, asked for favors, and moved things around as we could. We just found a way to persevere.

VMP did make it through this time and made its way to successful growth. However, a few years later, Matt decided he was ready for a change and stepped away from the company's day-to-day operations. I asked him, "Fast forward thirty to forty years. What does success in your career look like?"

After eight years leading VMP, I was burnt out. The line between VMP and myself was blurred, and I knew that was a dangerous place to be. I remember going to my therapist while I was in transition and just unloading on her. I told her how confused I was, how lost I felt, and how unsure of and ashamed of myself I was.

She asked if I have ever heard of EMDR[20] therapy. It's a form of trauma therapy. The way she defined trauma is when something happens, and you don't have the emotional maturity to know how to process it. So, it sticks in your short-term memory. Through EMDR, you are able to reprocess those memories and move them to your long-term memory bank, and experience relief.

I had a pretty good life up until that point and couldn't recall much 'trauma.' She went on to say that it's not always big things. It can be little things, often things that happened to you when you were a kid, whether they're significant or insignificant. And those experiences can affect who you are and how you show up in ways that you wouldn't really imagine. She recommended we try EMDR as a way to identify the sources of my

---

[20] Eye movement desensitization and reprocessing therapy.

insecurities and to reprogram those memories.

As I was reliving these memories, my therapist asked me to identify somebody that could be there with me as a safety guard. The first time that I did it, I just imagined this man. He looked like Al Borland from Home Improvement. I had never seen him before, though he faintly resembled an older version of myself.

He became a person that was there with me, comforting me throughout this whole process. It sounds crazy, but I developed a relationship with this man. He was someone I could access on a semi-regular basis. I felt like I knew him, and he knew me. Over time, I saw him as both a fully actualized version of myself and as God showing up in my life in very real ways.

I can recall one specific instance. I'm processing a memory, and he shows up. I tell him I don't know what to do or where to go. I was flustered because I didn't know what I was supposed to do with my life or why I was here. He doesn't say anything; he just lets me go. Eventually, he puts he cups his hands and shows them to me. They're super worn out and leathered. Clearly beaten up from a life's worth of work.

He says to me, "Do you see my hands? Do you see what they've done? This is why you're here."

This has been a profound image for me. It's helped me understand that part of success, part of why I'm here, is to do the work. In some ways, the results don't matter, nor does it really matter what the work is.

It's simply the willingness to show up and to trudge forward, despite whatever obstacles lay in front of me. It was a call to build, to make, to create. And through creation, I would have the ability to affect my world in some way. But I must be willing to get my hands dirty.

And so, when I'm 78 years old, and I'm reflecting on my life, I'm going to be looking at my hands. I'm going to look to them to remind me of all that I've done, and I will determine success, not by any objective metric, but by how weathered they are.

Chapter 32

Ian Miller

Ian has been a touring musician, playing piano, for the past ten years. Currently, he tours with country artist Brett Eldredge. Ian is also a producer. Like many young producers, he started with a studio in his bedroom. Ian and I had our conversation in the newly (almost) completed Roasted Bean Studio that he built in the garage behind the home he owns in Nashville.

I've always been kind of a tinkerer. For a while, I thought about doing something in computer science. My dad likes to tell a story about how I took his desktop computer apart when I was maybe 8 years old. There were pieces all over the floor as he walked into the room with a look of horror on his face. But somehow, I managed to identify each part and reconstruct the computer. I think that mindset – trying to solve the puzzle with the pieces you have available – has played into where I am now as a producer as well as a performer.

To me, there are two sides of music. The performance side, which is the energy of being on a stage in front of an audience. A lot of people don't have performance experience early on, but I was playing in dive bars until well into the AM on Friday nights as a 15-year-old kid! And then there's the cranial act of playing and creating with other people; that is, the exchange of ideas and the musical interaction between peers. I experience this the most while I'm in the studio or while playing more complex music live.

For years, I recorded in my bedroom in Nashville. I could make a great record, but occasionally you'd have to mind the unmade bed or dirty laundry shoved in a corner. I've always loved the magic of tracking a full band live, so at I certain point I felt stifled by the bedroom space. One of the reasons I bought the house in which I currently live is because it had a detached garage that was prime for converting into a separate recording studio. I felt that, for the first time ever, I could achieve my musical goals while charging what my services were worth.

This studio has been a brainchild of mine since I moved to Nashville. The first time I ever recorded, semi-legitimately, was with one of my oldest musical buddies; we recorded his little four-song EP in the attic of a house in St. Louis. I first discovered my love for recording in that experience. I would also write jingles as a teenager for my dad, who owned a small marketing firm. The first real recording computer and software I ever owned came from composing a jingle in exchange for a laptop.

Possibly my favorite part of being in the studio is taking the seed of an idea for a song and growing it to its final form. Whether I am playing or producing for other musicians, it's amazing to see the process develop. But it can also be exhausting when I'm deep in the weeds of a project. I've found that touring, in the right setting, frees my mind from that and creates balance in my career. The studio provides me with the creative expression part and the live side provides me with the performance part. Being up on stage, playing in front of an audience, feeling that kind of energy and adrenaline – that's something I just don't get when I'm sitting in a studio for eight hours. You just don't get the same kind of rush in the studio as you do when you're on stage.

However, when you're out playing the same show seventy or eighty times a year, it can get a little mundane. And sometime, you feel like you're going out there, checking the box, and moving on to another city just to see the insides of another locker room. So, pursuing a healthy balance between studio and live sides of music has been an ongoing goal of mine, with one side fueling the passion for the other. And for a while, I think I had it. But it inevitably skews in one direction or the other.

It's finding the right amount of work I want to put into each side. And right now, it's shifted primarily towards the touring side, to the point where I've been questioning how much I want to play live going forward. I feel like this year is the first time I've truly believed in my abilities and in the value of my time, so that's exciting. I'm at the point where I'm not interested in going out in a van and trailer, touring for months on end. I'm entering a more mature phase of my career, which also has me examining my roles in each facet of my musical life and determining how I want to balance them.

Before COVID hit, I had been taking on a bunch of production and recording projects. But I overextended myself to the point where it felt like a cloud of never-ending work was continuously hanging over my head. Additionally, some of the negatives that accompany working from home were impacting me - the constant distractions, the lack of separation between personal and work life. I fell into a dark place for a while because I was focusing less about on the creative process of making music and more on the stress of having strangers walk into my bedroom every other day. And, you know, the judgment that comes with that. It felt like a constant breach of privacy. That lack of separation was unconsciously seeping into relationships and even affecting my motivation to work.

So, I started ramping that down in preparation for constructing the new space. And for the past couple of years, I've been so bogged down by this construction that it became hard to see the light at the end of the tunnel. On top of that, with a global pandemic shutting the world down for two-plus years, there was no touring to bring me out of this headspace. It put me in a kind of a dark spot with music. But the first couple of times I recorded in here, I felt myself being more connected to the music again. It's honestly been this perspective shift of, again, figuring out what I do with my career and with music.

I haven't had much of a work-life balance over the past ten years. Somebody asked me yesterday what my hobbies are. I like to throw the baseball around sometimes, or I'll go and play video games for a while just to sort of reset. But I don't have too many other hobbies besides playing music because, at its best, it's something I love to do more than almost anything else. I feel myself going through these huge valleys and peaks of taking exorbitant amounts of work, then burning out. And then taking a week or two off, just removing myself a little bit, to find the itch again. That process has repeated itself pretty consistently for ten years. So, I think that it has given me some insight into needing to make a change earlier rather than later. Do I want to start a family? When do I want to start a family? What sort of things do I need to be looking at to provide a foundation for that? What am I looking for in my most important relationships? How do I want to live my life?

From the beginning, my parents have always been extremely supportive of what I've done. And I cannot emphasize that enough. That really set the stage for everything. They've been there to congratulate me on the triumphs and encourage me during the pitfalls. I continuously try to incorporate my dad's entrepreneurial spirit and work ethic and my mom's thoughtfulness and selflessness into my life. I certainly wouldn't be where I am now without them.

Beyond my parents, there have been a couple friends and mentors who have inspired me with the way their careers and family lives intersect. One of them is Drew Holcomb, the man that seems to be able take on the world, yet still be truly present for his family. To be on the road a lot and still be there for his kids' soccer games. To be able to bring the kids out to shows. To see how involved he is in their lives. He does a tour every year where it's him and Ellie[21]. They'll bring the kids on the tour bus and make it a whole experience! And beyond music, he is a businessman as well. He's involved in several ventures, including a whiskey venture with Peyton Manning and many golf endeavors. But music and family are at the core. So, seeing that and knowing it's possible to still be involved and be happy and be present, it's been amazing.

Another colleague of mine, Jordan Lehning, has a studio similar to mine; it's a converted garage behind his house. Sometimes in the middle of sessions, his kids will run out and interact with whoever's inside and then go back to school or whatever they were working on. He makes them feel included but never to the detriment of the session or to the point of distraction. It's encouraging to witness this firsthand knowing that I may be in a similar scenario someday.

At this point, I think what it comes down to is recognizing time as a precious commodity and understanding the tremendous value of achieving a healthy balance between all the important parts of life. I certainly haven't found it yet, but I'm working on it.

---

[21] Drew Holcomb's wife

Chapter 33

Janice Dotti Townsend

When Janice was in college, she dreamed of someday starting a coffee shop. Little did she know that it would happen much more quickly than she ever imagined.

I graduated with this big business plan for a coffee shop but no money to put the plan into action. I also had no professional job because it was the beginning of 2008, and there were no jobs due to the financial crisis. So, I ended up moving home, which is always a little ego death. I did some odd jobs around town and dreamed of opening a coffee shop.

Even still, my family encouraged me to pursue starting the business, saying, "You should at least look at spaces because everything's really affordable right now."

I worked with a family friend who was a commercial real estate agent and looked at some different spots. Long story short, it all ended up happening a lot quicker than I thought it was going to happen.

I was super scared, but it felt like the right thing for me. It was what I needed to be doing, and I needed to take that step. But I was young; I was twenty-two when I opened the shop.

The narrative in my head said, "If you want to do this, there's an opportunity to do it now. No one else is doing this. Rent is affordable, so you can do this for much less than it would cost in an up economy."

But it was also tricky because of the down economy. Things were cheaper, but we were also the first craft coffee shop in the area and used a fair-trade model. People were used to the quick "corporate coffee shop experience" where you just go to the drive-through to get your 20oz sugary latte. We had a lot of work to do to educate and allow our customers to experience craft coffee, which was a big hurdle in the beginning. It was a slow ramp-up—very, very slow.

The first two years were really hard, and we lost money for the first year. I worked 60 to 80 hours a week but had less money than when I started, which is not a good feeling. I lived on the cheap and worked all the time.

ENTREPRENEURIAL VOICES

Most days, I opened the shop alone, arriving around 5:30 am and finishing my bar shift around 3:00 pm. On top of that, I would do all of my owner duties, including payroll, scheduling, ordering, marketing, and inventory. I was also learning as I went, so I was making a lot of mistakes. The hardest thing for me was not knowing how to manage people yet; I only knew how to manage myself. But we were building this really cool community as I was learning how to build a business.

It was really hard for the first few years, but I kept going. Had failure been an option, I probably would have given up on more than a few occasions. I see something interesting now, especially when people take investment money, and it's not their money - they don't have skin in the game, and they sometimes give up at the first sign of hardship. I didn't have that option. So, I had to keep going. I'm really glad I did because things eventually started to change.

I started making some quality hires as I learned more about what questions to ask and what to avoid when hiring. I was also able to retain people better as we grew and be more competitive with pay. As we grew, we started to have this cool team cohesion that we hadn't had in the early days. And that's when it got fun—when I felt like I was working with a team instead of just keeping the ship afloat by myself.

***

The basic model for Roots was a retail coffee shop. It's all about lots and lots of small ticket purchases. While it was a quantity game of how many people we could get through the doors every day, we really wanted to balance that with inviting people to stay and have an experience.

We were having struggles with not having enough places for people to sit at certain times of the day and customers buying one thing and staying for twelve hours. So, we started a café barista shift, where a barista would go around with an iPad and check in on people. We shifted our afternoons and evenings to more of a table service model, and at the same time, we added beer and wine as well as more food options. Ironically, in 2020, right before the pandemic, we launched a little campaign called "Share Your Table." We had these coasters printed; if you want to share your table, put the coaster up that says "Share." But then the pandemic happened, and everything just got shut down, requiring some pivots.

We started in a 2000-square-foot space in North Richland Hills, which is in the suburbs between Dallas and Fort Worth, in 2009. When my husband and I moved to Fort Worth in 2016, I knew I wanted the second location of Roots to be in our new community, but I also knew I did not want to be a renter forever. When I calculated how much I had spent in rent at the North Richland Hills location over 7 years, I realized owning the real estate made much more sense if possible. In order to do that, my husband and I purchased land in an urban neighborhood that was being redeveloped after a major road reconstruction. In order to make the cost of the land make sense, we had to make the building multi-use, so the coffeehouse ended up just being a small portion of the building, and the rest was office space. It took nearly three years from buying the land to opening our doors, but when the project was finished, we owned a beautiful 7500-square-foot modern building about a mile from downtown Fort Worth. That project could be the subject of another whole interview; many lessons were learned.

My favorite season of owning Roots was the season leading up to opening the second shop. I had a wonderful leadership team and great people who I loved working with. We dreamed, brainstormed, and problem-solved together. Our team felt really healthy, and it was a lot of fun. We opened our second location in December 2019.

And then, months after we opened our second location, COVID hit. We were fortunate because we had so many people excited about the second location and a strong customer base from our original location. We were well supported during the pandemic. Because the new location was the same business and not a separate new business, we were eligible for the grants and PPP[22] funding. It was not easy, but doable. We were fortunate, but it still took a toll.

Managing the new norms that came with COVID entailed pivoting our business model to to-go only overnight, keeping up with local mandates and best practices, becoming experts in cleanliness and minimizing contact, keeping our staff well cared for, and constant communication. Later in the pandemic, during different COVID waves, we would have exposures and sickness leading to reduced hours and closures. During certain times, there just weren't enough resources to keep the shop open without overburdening the staff. Those were tough weeks.

As COVID became the new normal, I was trying to find the spot for our

---

[22] Paycheck Protection Program

third location. I felt that we had to keep growing to keep developing the team, offering better full-time positions to baristas who wanted to stay with the company long-term. I had many qualified people who wanted to be in management, but I didn't have jobs for them. I felt compelled to keep going. But every time I went to see a space and thought it might be a good fit, I could not get any traction from the building owner. I tried to put LOI's on three different spaces and they were all rejected. It seemed like the universe was trying to tell me something.

And so, around late 2021, I felt fatigued from the pandemic and business ownership. At this point, I had owned and operated the business for twelve years and I didn't even really realize that I could sell it. I don't know if that makes sense, but I didn't even realize it was an option. I was talking to a friend who was telling me how he was considering selling his business. I was like, "Wait. Can I do that?" And it was almost like this deep exhale.

I continued to mull it over throughout the holiday season. We were with family in New York for Christmas, and on Christmas Day, one of my managers called me and said that one employee had COVID, and another one was exposed. We spent 2 hours on Christmas Day reworking the schedules so we could open the next day. I had this very strong feeling that I did not want to be doing this next Christmas. But I still wasn't sure I wanted to sell.

The two weeks that followed were some of the hardest we've ever been through. That's when we got broken into. That's when the equipment went down. That's when half my staff was out with COVID. We had to shorten our hours. We were having trouble getting supplies. Everything was expensive. This was like the confirmation that it was time for me to get out before I was totally depleted.

I wanted to sell it while I still loved it. I still very much loved it. But I also felt like there was something else I needed to do. So, in January of 2022, I put the business on the market.

I did not use the broker. I used a local listing site. I also have a friend who runs a coffee school in Arlington and I reached out to him because he meets people who want to open coffee shops all the time. Between contacting him and the listing, I had four offers within about a month. It was very validating and somewhat surprising to me. The potential buyers were saying things like, "We love Roots! This would be a dream opportunity." Finally, I had options.

I wanted to make sure that a future owner continued Roots with values similar to how I was running the business and the community values we had created over the years. The people I ended up choosing were a local entrepreneurial couple who already had a food service business and a couple of other businesses around pets. I really appreciated their vision. They also were the only ones saying they would provide a full health insurance plan for the staff, which is something I hadn't been able to afford with just two locations. They had experience. They had a team already in place. They weren't the highest offer, but they were the most qualified people.

I look at those early days and wonder, "How did I do that?" It was a lot of my life. I owned Roots for thirteen and a half years, so it was a huge portion of my life. Even when I was on vacation or off for the day, I was always on call. Actually, I've had a couple of moments since selling where I'll hear my phone ringing, and I'm like, "Now what's going on? Who needs me?" That response is still trained in me. It's taking time for me to mellow out after all of those high-stress years. But I'm absolutely glad I did it. It taught me lessons that I don't think I could have learned in any other way and made me who I am.

The first month after selling, my husband and I went on a road trip. We just left town, and we went west to see friends. It felt like a detox. I got back from the road trip and have spent the last year just taking time to explore more creative endeavors. I've been writing. I'm getting my yoga teacher training certification. I'm working on a couple of ideas, but nothing business-related. I'm just taking some time to explore what it's like to be a human again.

Chapter 34

Tony Bakker

Tony Bakker moved to Nashville from Holland, Michigan, to study music and find his place in the music business. That journey would lead him to co-found an online guitar lesson website, Six String Country, and eventually, move back to Michigan.

This would have been in 2012. I had been noticing all these guitar lesson videos on YouTube, and some were getting a lot of hits. And I thought, "You know, I can teach these songs pretty easily." I focused mainly on country, and much to my surprise, I started getting a lot of views. As the channel was picking up, I started to wonder if we did things more professionally and gave people more resources, you know, sheet music, tabs, chord charts, if people would pay for it on a subscription basis. I had worked in the publishing field for almost a decade at that point. I knew that that would be illegal unless we got the licenses. I didn't really know where to start with that.

I took my friend Ryan Beuschel out for sushi. Ryan knew all the publishers in Nashville and had a really good reputation. He thought my idea could have some legs. We met with people at several publishing companies and asked, "Is it possible? Would you give us a license for something like this?" If they would have said no, we would have just had to find a different idea or just keep doing our jobs.

Everyone seemed to say, "You know, we have ways to do this, and it's something that we think we need." Ryan knew the people at the publishing companies well enough that he knew they weren't pulling his leg. And he felt pretty confident that we could get some deals done.

And so, that's when we started Six String Country. Neither of us had a lot of money, so we agreed to keep working our jobs and moonlight the business. So, after work and on weekends, we'd be working on Six String Country.

We had to figure out how to get enough money to build the initial website. We had some different options. Some of the people that we talked to in the music business said, "Hey, we think we have some people that would probably be interested in investing in this." And then they explained that until they got paid back, they were going to own a large percentage of the business. Then, after we pay them back, we'd own more of the business.

Thankfully, my dad started his own business a long time ago and had an entrepreneurial bent to him. But he is also not a huge risk-taker. I had 65% of the money that we needed in our savings account. My dad said, and I'll never forget the way he said it, "You know, Tony, I have the money I can loan you, but I don't have it to lose." Which essentially meant to me it doesn't matter if this company goes bankrupt. I'm going to have to get a second job or something and pay my dad back one way or the other. It wasn't a gift. But also, he was very generous in that he didn't make us give him a percentage of the business. It was a five-year loan that we had paid back in 18 months. I'll always be appreciative of my mom and dad for doing that.

Ryan has always done Six String Country part-time. I was the only one who would be quitting my job. I tried to time it to about when the website would be ready to go, and we could launch. I tried to give myself about one to two months of not working so I could really focus on making content. But I didn't want it to be more than that because I didn't want to run out of money. We ended up timing it pretty well. I had a fantastic boss and a mentor, almost like a second father. He was my only boss since I graduated college. And so, I was really nervous about telling him because I was afraid I was going to disappoint him. I think it did disappoint him a little bit. But he was gracious about it. And we're still very tight to this day. I gave him a month's notice. And then, when that month was up, I was self-employed, not making any money.

Bethany[23] was just so supportive the whole way. I think I would have been pretty nervous if I were her, but she always thought it was a good idea. She liked the idea of the flexibility of being my own boss. She had a good job, too. In the worst-case scenario, we could have probably scraped by, at least for a while. I was quite nervous. But at the same time, I was so excited about it that my excitement masked the nervousness a little bit.

We launched with about fourteen lessons. Now we have over 900! I've learned more and more that people are interested in what's new, and you have to have a compelling amount of content for them to sign up for something like this. At the time, the quality of our content was very compelling, but the quantity was not. That was keeping me up at night. I was busting out lessons as best as I could. If you use the actual song from

---

[23] Bethany (Beth) is Tony's wife.

the record, you have to pay the record label for the master in addition to the publishing. And that was a dealbreaker. We decided we'd rerecord the tracks from the ground up. You're learning the song, recording the jam along with it on the videos, and editing all those videos. Then, I had to do all the sheet music, the tabs, and the chord charts. That's how I did it for maybe two or three years before we had anyone else do a lesson for us as an instructor. I was probably doing 60 hours plus most weeks just to get the content. We just had to get that compelling amount of content up there.

We launched with zero subscribers. Our goal was to get three subscribers a day, which would get us to 1,000 subscribers by the end of the year. If we got to 1,000 subscribers, we could pay our bills. I could be making about what I was making before. We hit 1,000 in about nine months.

It just felt like a real weight was lifted. Until you get to that point where it's going to sustain itself and you can support your family, you still have that weight on your shoulders. But when we hit that goal, it was a freeing moment, and I felt like it was going to make it. And then, after that first year, it really started snowballing. But strangely, at that time, we weren't really spending any money on marketing. It was all just mainly coming from YouTube.

So, you decided to leave Nashville and move back to Michigan in the midst of all this?

Well, there are a couple of reasons for moving back. Number one, Beth and I were interested in starting a family. And all of our family, parents, siblings, and grandparents, live about thirty minutes from where we live now in Michigan. Our nieces and nephews were getting older, and we were missing more and more stuff. We just thought it was time to move back.

The other reason to move back was that I pretty much cleaned out our bank account down to a few thousand dollars. Part of the plan was to sell our house in Nashville and buy a much cheaper house in Michigan. Kind of gave us a little padding. And that's exactly what we did. We did great selling our house and got a pretty nice little house for under $100,000. And that really helped us to stay afloat. I didn't pay myself from the business for about six or eight months. So that was kind of a key component to finding a way to get some extra money to live on.

There was the financial component of being able to provide for my family. But almost as important, the idea of being my own boss was very attractive to me. Having a flexible job and paying close attention to work/life balance. I knew in the short term that my balance wouldn't be very good, but long term, that is what is important to me. Having the flexibility to make my own decisions about my business and take vacations when I wanted to. If I want to mow the lawn at 10:00 in the morning and work until six or seven, know I can do that. Just the flexibility of having complete control over every aspect of my life was driving a lot of starting a business.

I never thought we'd have anywhere close to this many subscribers. We have people subscribing in over 40 countries. I just didn't realize how many people there were out there that would be interested in this. Another thing that surprised me is how well I've gotten to know some of my customers, even on an online platform that's subscription-based. I've become friends with many of them. I've gone to lunch with them. They come to my shows when I play my music in Michigan, and I've developed some really meaningful relationships. I really love interacting with customers.

My business relationship with Ryan has exceeded my expectations. Some people say, "Don't get a partner! You never know how that's going to go. It can be a real headache." But it never has been with Ryan. And I don't want to jinx it, but we've never had a big argument about anything. We love talking about strategy and how we can grow in different ways. It's been so rewarding just to have somebody to walk through that with, rather than always having to only trust your own gut. We've been good sounding boards for each other.

We've been approached by a couple of private equity groups. We went down a deep dive with one and were pretty close to a deal. They had sent us a letter of intent. We loosely said, "Okay, we're on board with this, but we still need to do our due diligence, take it to our lawyer, and all that kind of thing." And at the end of the day, we didn't do it. It just didn't feel like the right time, didn't feel like the right number. And the deal was kind of funny in some ways to us. But it was an interesting process to go through. And it did tell us that, at least, somebody out there thinks it's worth paying money for.

I was thinking about the three principles I try to live by: know yourself, change or die, and everything matters. The know yourself part would be to know what I'm good at and what I'm not good at and try to stay in my lane. And if I'm not good at something, find somebody who can do that for us. Change or die. Technology changes, and customers' expectations change. We always have to stay in touch with our customers and figure out what they want. And then, everything matters. The attention to detail -- the fonts, the colors, the user experience. Are the tabs all correct? Is the chord chart correct? We try really hard to keep those three things in mind to make sure somebody wants to pull out their credit card and pay us for lessons.

Chapter 35

Craig Irving

Craig Irving grew up in San Diego, where his parents encouraged him to become resourceful and entrepreneurial at a young age. In the early 1980s, Craig attended college at the University of Southern California. He majored in Entrepreneurship, which was a new area of study at that time. After graduation, he entered the world of commercial real estate, where he soon channeled his entrepreneurial spirit.

I saw a niche that had not been fulfilled in commercial real estate, and I went after it. Back in the eighties, the way commercial real estate brokers made a living was by representing landlords. They have the listing on the building, they fill it up, they work on renewals, expansions, and whatever else within that building. That's how business was conducted.

When I got onto my first high-rise listing working for my mentor, I learned everything about that building. I learned every aspect of high-rise office buildings, knowing them better than the listing brokers and their owners. You would think, why, why would I learn all that? My whole career, I never wanted to not have an answer to a question. I was going to put myself out there as a real estate professional and an expert, and I wanted to take pride in what I did for a living. There were so many boneheads out there that just went through the motions, glorified tour guides. And yeah, many were moderately successful. But to look at yourself in the mirror and say, "I am a master of my craft!" That's what I wanted to be.

And so, I learned the trivia about these buildings. Who is the developer, who was the owner, and who financed it? How much per square foot did it cost to build? Did it trade hands? When did it trade hands? Who were the original owners? Who were the second owners? What was the cost basis of the buildings? What was included in the operating expenses? What was not included? If it was net of utilities, what were the utility costs, tenant improvements, contractors, and everything about the buildings? Not only did I learn about the buildings, but I also learned about all my competitors because I wanted to be able to outsell all my competition.

One day these really nice people said, "We're going to go look at two other buildings. I said, "Can I go with you?" They kind of looked at me like that was kind of a weird question but said I could go with them.

I was somewhat quiet. I listened to the other brokers. We went and looked at the other two buildings. Afterward, I said, "If I were you, these are the things I would be looking at." They were impressed.

I had that "aha" moment, and I thought, "I'm really good at this. I know more about the competitors' buildings than they know because they're just lazy. I can really help a tenant out. Plus, tenants are not real estate experts. They are marketing firms, law firms, accounting firms, and a myriad of other office space consumers. They didn't know anything about commercial real estate. And it's David versus Goliath. Some nice people come through, and they don't know anything about my building, and I'm ripping them off. I'm charging them $0.50 more a foot than market because they don't know any better. A big company, maybe a big insurance company, owns this building. Whether it's a $0.50 or $0.05 difference, it's not going to change the owners lives. But for this tenant, it is going to change *theirs.*"

I had no interest in living the rest of my business life ripping tenants off. I wanted to represent the tenant, and I wanted to go after the landlords and grind the crap out of them. Nobody was doing it at the time.

After working at a large, traditional brokerage firm for five years, I went to my partner and said, "I'm leaving, and I want you to come with me. I'm not representing landlords anymore. I'm going to go out and represent tenants. Hope you come with me." I was 27. He agreed to come with me, and I was the junior partner.

Now, I'm at five years in the business by this time. I was doing everything for this guy. He was on "Easy Street." I had learned enough about the business, but I didn't have the gray hair that he had. So that was one disadvantage that I had, at least initially. You know, who's this pimply-faced kid coming in here? And so, we left. He was their top producer. They were so upset that we were leaving. And I remember my exit interview with the president telling me that I'd be back begging for my job in six months. And I smiled at him and said, "Well, you're just giving me more motivation to make sure that I'm successful." Upon hearing of my planned departure, many brokers within the company provided their advice saying, "You are a fool! Craig, you're such a nice young man, and you're going to fail." And I just smiled and just said, "Just keep stoking the fire."

I knew there was a market for it because I knew how much of a need I was fulfilling for tenants. A couple of companies in New York were doing strictly tenant representation firms, but none in California. I had no mentor and no roadmap for developing my business. Somebody asked me a question about waiver of subrogation in a lease document early in my new career, and I didn't know what the hell that was. But you know what? I had an answer the next time they asked me. I was getting questions that I certainly had no answer for, but it would just fire me up and motivate me to reach a point where I would have an answer to *any* question regarding commercial real estate.

I learned about the central business district inside and out. I walked into every high rise to see who was on the directories in the lobbies. I wrote down all the tenants' names and what floors they were on. And then I went to the public library. There was a business publication called the Daily Transcripts that published leasing notes every Tuesday and Thursday for the entire county. And it would tell me so-and-so leased 12,000 square feet at 1010 Second Avenue for five years, and it would list a little bit more information. I bought a computer database software system and developed a database. I read the Daily Transcripts cover-to-cover, twice forward and backward. I remember going to my mentor and saying, "Write down every single thing you want to know about a tenant. Business name, what they do, who the managing partner, the president, and the CEO are. Are they publicly traded or private businesses? Who's the office manager? What's their square footage? When's their lease expiration date." And this was back in the day when I was one of the first brokers to even own a computer, just prior to the dawn of the fax machine, with cell phones non-existent.

I went to the white pages and looked at every single tenant and all of their names, building by building. I think there were 15 high rises at the time in downtown San Diego. And then, I would do mid-rises and low rises. I would call them up on the phone and kill them with kindness. I would tell them I had some questions as I was building a database and ask if they could help me out. And I tried to fill out every single question, and then I put it all into a database. I now had a very rough database, but a pretty damn good one. Now, what do I do with it?

I started calling these tenants up. And, you know, a lot of them didn't know when their lease expiration dates were. My job was to get a meeting and sell my services. And that's how it all started.

From 1989 until 1991, I did all the work. I was the one getting all the clients. I went to my partner and said, "Our splits aren't fair." He would come in at ten in the morning, read the newspaper, then want to go to lunch and hear what I was working on, and then leave at three. I felt like I had paid him back in spades for what he had done for me as a mentor. He agreed to change our split. Six months later, he was so stressed out about life. He had no business being in this high-intensity business. I said, "John, you need to get out of this business. You're going to have a heart attack because, you know, somebody put mayonnaise on your sandwich that you ordered for lunch." He would just blow up over little things.

And he said, "You know what? I'm actually leaving. I'm going to go take a job up in L.A. and mellow out for the rest of my life." And so, it was an amicable split. I was on my own. I was fine with that. I was totally comfortable. I was kicking ass.

People started to say, "Who's this young kid kicking ass? He seems to be representing half of the tenants in downtown San Diego." Over the years, I exploited that other brokers had a conflict of interest: you cannot serve two masters. Their Achilles heel was that they worked for a big firm, and they represented half the buildings in town. How can you represent the tenants' best interests? That was a winning pitch for me. If there was a contest and it was a level playing field, I won 90% of the time. All I had to do was get in front of a tenant, and I would get their business.

We had just represented the City of San Diego. We competed with 19 other firms, and we got that account. It was a huge account. I represented them for over ten years. I was their exclusive tenant broker. I just skyrocketed from there and grew my firm. We grew that firm to be the absolute dominant tenant rep firm in San Diego. For probably 15 years in a row, we had 70 to 90% market share in the central business district, and every year we would be so angry that we didn't have 100%!

I was a walking encyclopedia of the downtown market. I knew where every tenant was. I knew everything about those tenants. I knew everything about every building. Tenants stayed downtown. That was where the courthouses were. That was where the Big Eight accounting firms were. That was where all the law firms were. And so, people either stayed where they were for years or would move across the street into the shiny new building.

Pretty quickly after I started representing tenants, a couple other guys popped up in the market, you know, one-offs. And then, I noticed that the bigger firms were changing. They would have a tenant in their building that wanted to expand, and there was no expansion space in their building. So, a guy from a big brokerage, would say, "Well, you know, there's space over across the street. Let me take you over there." That started happening. If you look at the central business district, there were 10 million square feet of tenants. For a time, 8 million of them were my clients. The majority of my business was repeat business and referrals. As time went on, I did less and less cold calling. I didn't need to. My reputation spoke for itself. I had to book a business, and I had referrals, and I didn't need to go beat the bushes.

It became harder to compete. My market shrank. The GSA[24] was already off the table. That was 20% of the marketplace. But then what started happening was the large national brokerages went to the corporate headquarters of Fortune 500 companies and said, "We'll take care of your leases throughout the country. We have people, and we have offices in every city. Let us represent that." So, all of a sudden, the big eight accounting firms, the national law firms, the national marketing firms, and most big companies were off the table. So that 80% went to 60% and then it kept declining. There was a smaller, smaller pool.

But I did what I did, and then I left because the market shifted, and it was out of my control. It didn't matter how good I was. The market shrank because so many tenants were off the market because of new global tenant rep firms or tenant rep divisions within the big brokerage firms. During the last eight years of my career, I was approached by a lot of the big companies to buy my company and run their tenant rep divisions. I just had no interest. I could not sell my soul to the devil.

I got out. I was just I was burned out. Been there, done that. And I didn't need to work anymore. You reach a point in life where, you know, I don't need an airplane, and I don't need a fancy yacht. And my kids are all taken care of, and I don't have any debts. And it was time for me to just say, "I'm done. I've done it all. I don't need to do it anymore." And I'm going to go to Tennessee, drive a tractor, and do other things that I want to enjoy in life. Was that a hard transition to zero? It was the easiest and most rewarding thing for me.

---

[24] The Government Services Administration (GSA) manages federal government office space nationally.

EPILOGUE

In the Introduction, I said this book is a series of stories about lessons learned. I also said that I learned from talking to the entrepreneurs in this book. I learned new lessons and had many old lessons reaffirmed.

In reflecting on the stories about vision, purpose, and culture, I was reminded of the diversity of the motivations that drive entrepreneurs. There is a common myth I hear over and over that entrepreneurship is really only about "the money." However, when we look at the hard data about business ownership, entrepreneurship is not a very rational way to secure a healthy income and build wealth. More entrepreneurs fall short or even fail in pursuing their financial goals. In reality, many entrepreneurs persevere with their businesses in spite of the financial rewards (or lack of rewards) their businesses yield for them. The motivations that drive entrepreneurs include an incredible array of goals. However, money is very far down the list for most business owners. This book includes people seeking a more independent lifestyle than a job typically offers. For others, entrepreneurship is a path to impact a higher purpose tied to the business owner's life story. Some entrepreneurs want to prove they can build a common business in not-so-common ways. No two entrepreneurs in this book were driven by the same motivation. I learned that to really understand an entrepreneur, you must dig much deeper than their business model and their financial statements.

This book offers some inspirational stories about the perseverance it takes to build a successful business. I heard stories about overcoming personal challenges, financial adversity, nay-sayers, nefarious people, and fickle markets. When putting myself in their shoes, I am not sure I would have had the stick-to-itiveness required by many entrepreneurs who shared their stories with me. Even some of the business owners in this book, whom I have known throughout their entrepreneurial journeys, dealt with challenges I never knew they had to endure. Many simply firmed their resolve and marched forward without a complaint or excuse.

One of my current favorite books about entrepreneurship is Heart, Smarts, Guts, and Luck by Tjan, Harrington, and Hsieh. The authors found that when looking at what leads to entrepreneurial success, no matter how passionate, brilliant, and courageous an entrepreneur may be, luck always plays a significant part in any business owner's story. Indeed, a stroke of luck can come into play along the way for many businesses. What was amazing to me was how often luck, or as I like to call it, serendipity, plays such an important role at the beginning of so many entrepreneurial stories!

I have spent a good part of my career helping young, idealistic aspiring entrepreneurs. My own entrepreneurial journey began at a very young age. I hope and pray that our culture continues to lead many young people into a career as entrepreneurs. They help fuel the engine of business formation that drives our economy forward. Without young entrepreneurs, I fear that our economy will stagnate. The stories of people starting their work lives as business owners instill hope in me for our collective futures.

Balance, the topic of the book's final section, in many ways, is a mirror image of the first section on vision, purpose, and success. The entrepreneurs throughout this book, particularly in the final section, affirm that success is so much more than just financial outcomes for most business owners. However, finding a path to the non-financial goals important to most business owners is much easier said than done. The stories also make clear that owning a business can be like holding onto the tail of a tiger. It often takes us along for a wild ride and can be exceedingly difficult to control.

Hearing other entrepreneurs' stories is one of my favorite aspects of my entrepreneurial life. I have used them to inform how I have managed my own businesses. I have built them into my lectures, my coaching, and my books to reinforce important lessons for the entrepreneurs I have helped along the way. I hope you have found the stories in this book to be both instructive and inspirational.

ABOUT THE AUTHOR

Dr. Jeff Cornwall has spent more than forty years as a serial entrepreneur and educator of entrepreneurs. In the 1970s, he started several small businesses and was involved in various family ventures. In the late 1980s, following several years in academics, Dr. Cornwall co-founded Atlantic Behavioral Health Systems in Raleigh, NC, and spent nearly a decade leading the company as President/CEO. After growing to more than 300 employees, he and his partners sold most of their healthcare holdings. After the sale, Dr. Cornwall decided it was time to return to the classroom to share his experience and knowledge with aspiring entrepreneurs.

In his academic career, Dr. Cornwall held faculty positions at several universities. He received national awards for his curriculum development and teaching. In 2013, the United States Association of Small Business and Entrepreneurship named Dr. Cornwall the National Entrepreneurship Educator of the Year. Upon his retirement from Belmont University, he was named Professor Emeritus of Entrepreneurship.

He is currently the co-founder and president of Entrepreneurial Mind, LLC, a content creation company. Its courses are centered around professional and personal development for entrepreneurs and small business owners. The company provides digital education content through partnerships with online educational platforms.

He has published ten books on entrepreneurship. He also published numerous articles on entrepreneurship and small business throughout his career.

ENTREPRENEURIAL VOICES

www.ingramcontent.com/pod-product-compliance
Lightning Source LLC
Chambersburg PA
CBHW052153220526
45471CB00004B/1651